Memories from
the Twentieth
Century

T0345490

The Italian List

SERIES EDITOR: ALBERTO TOSCANO

Luigi Pintor

Memories from the Twentieth Century

TRANSLATED BY GREGORY ELLIOTT

EDITED AND INTRODUCED
BY ALBERTO TOSCANO

LONDON NEW YORK CALCUTTA

Seagull Books, 2018

Luigi Pintor, *Servabo*
© Bollati Boringhieri editore, Torino, 1991

Luigi Pintor, *La signora Kirchgessner*
© Bollati Boringhieri editore, Torino, 1998

Luigi Pintor, *Il nespolo*
© Bollati Boringhieri editore, Torino, 2001

First published in English translation by Seagull Books, 2013

Introduction © Alberto Toscano, 2013
Translation © Gregory Elliott, 2011

ISBN 978 0 8574 2 578 2

British Library Cataloguing-in-Publication Data
A catalogue record for this book is available from the British Library

Typeset by Seagull Books, Calcutta, India
Printed and bound by Maple Press, York, Pennsylvania, USA

CONTENTS

The experience of communist militancy in the twentieth century left deep if ambivalent traces on the genres of autobiography and memoir. Entrance into the communist movement could require the composition of narratives relating how class, consciousness and conversion had rallied an individual party member to the cause.[1] Inversely, repudiation of one's communist past frequently took a confessional mode, most clamorously in *The God that Failed,* though Cold War examples are legion. A number of prominent figures in *il manifesto*—the independent communist newspaper and political-intellectual project to which Luigi Pintor committed himself from 1969 until his death in 2003—have also recently produced important personal retrospects on their times and politics.[2]

---

1 See, for example, Marco Boarelli, *La fabbrica del passato. Autobiografie di militanti comunisti (1945–1956)* (Rome: Feltrinelli, 2007), a study of archives collecting short autobiographies that members of the Italian Communist Party (Partito Comunista Italiano or PCI) had to draft in the first postwar decade.

2 Rossana Rossanda's *The Comrade from Milan* (Romy Giuliani Clark trans., London: Verso, 2010)—with its accompanying

The three texts collected here depart considerably from prior templates. Formative political moments punctuate the prose, but, though Pintor doesn't repudiate his commitments, they are shorn of heroism, touched by a kind of irony that often verges on self-deprecation. Political acts and events are displaced by their proximity to the joys of Pintor's Sardinian childhood, as well as by the lacerating losses of his later years (the death of his wife, and, in quick succession, of his two adult children). This is not to say that, despite being increasingly estranged, as we move from *Servabo* through *Miss Kirchgessner* to the more fictional and aphoristic *The Medlar Tree*, the landmarks of his political biography cannot can be clearly identified: the death of his elder brother Giaime, literary scholar and resistance hero, in 1943;[3] his participation in partisan urban guerrilla against the Nazi Occupation in Rome, and subsequent

---

volume *Un viaggio inutile,* on an abortive party mission to Franco's Spain)—recounts her life in the PCI up to the expulsion of the *manifesto* group; Luciana Castellina's *La scoperta del mondo* (Rome: Nottetempo, 2011), revisits her youth diaries to retrace how a young woman of the bourgeoisie could have come to discover herself, and her world, through the prism of communist commitment, amid the tumult of the war and its aftermath; Lucio Magri's *The Tailor of Ulm* (Patrick Camiller trans., London: Verso, 2011) presents a critical panorama of the PCI's singular history, and its demise, from the perspective of a dissident militant who, like his other comrades, can be said to have never fully left the PCI, in spite of actual expulsions and unsparing criticisms. See also Gregory Elliott's review of Magri's book, 'Parti Pris' in *New Left Review* 75 (2012): 145–52.

3 On the figure of Giaime Pintor, see the collective volume, published in 2005 by manifestolibri, *Giaime Pintor e la sua generazione,*

arrest, torture and near execution in 1944; his work as a journalist in the PCI newspaper *l'Unità* in the two decades after the war;[4] election to the PCI's Central Committee in 1962, and the later dissident position in the party, culminating in his open opposition to the party's stance on the 1968 invasion of Czechoslovakia, and the expulsion of the *manifesto* group in 1969; stints in parliament in 1968 and 1987; the passage of *il manifesto*, whose founding had triggered the excommunication, from a journal to a newspaper.

But the form that these experiences receive and the light cast upon them are very distant from those of most communist memoirs. The first volume, *Servabo*, marks its place at the end of the short twentieth century, and follows closely upon the end of the PCI, whose shabby denouement Pintor dissected in the pages of *il manifesto*. But the way that it mediates personal and political experience is far more conflicted and oblique than could have been expected from such a public political figure as Pintor. The usual tropes of conversion and betrayal, awakening or delusion, are absent, and, though the leitmotifs of grief and futility

---

which includes reminiscences from Luigi, as well as political contemporaries of Giaime, alongside essays on his place as a Germanist literary scholar and critic, his political thought, and his role in the resistance.

4 As Phillip Willan observed, in his obituary in the *Guardian*: 'Pintor had a clear idea of the appropriate relationship between a periodical and the party it supported—like a swallow in the party's hand, he suggested, a hand that must not grip too tightly, lest the bird suffocate, nor too loosely, lest it fly away' (20 May 2003).

abound, they never announce a reconciliation with that world of capitalist modernization that Pintor spent his life writing against—as his very last editorial in *il manifesto*, against the invasion of Iraq, angrily testified. The despair that transpires from these pages, as Pintor's many assiduous readers in Italy knew, didn't attenuate but intensified the ethical and political intransigence that marked Pintor's writing and person, which is to say his style. As his *manifesto* comrade Rossana Rossanda put it, 'he passed away unreconciled'.

It is precisely around this question of style—best crystallized in the motto from *The Medlar Tree* 'synthesis is poetry'—that we can grasp the uniqueness of the link between writing, politics and experience in Pintor, in both their rare convergence and the shearing tension that always threatened to leave them sundered from one another, non-communicating. Pintor was widely recognized in Italy, by comrades and adversaries alike, as the best political editorialist of the postwar period.[5] And though the tenor and

---

5 Pintor never ceased to remark upon the ephemerality, or even futility, of the editorial as a mode of intervention. That said, the volumes that collect some of the 'pile twelve thousand calendar sheets high' (*Servabo*), made up by Pintor's front-page commentaries for *il manifesto,* not only make rewarding reading as exemplary specimens of journalistic and political style, they are also an indispensable accompaniment to the vicissitudes of the Italian polity in the last four decades. In particular, they serve as an acerbic chronicle of the virtually unalloyed mendaciousness and mediocrity of its political class. See *I corsivi del manifesto* (1976); *Parole al vento. Brevi cronache degli anni '80* (1990); *Politicamente scorretto. Cronache di un quinquennio 1996–2001* (2001); *Punto e a capo. Scritti sul manifesto 2001–2003* (2004).

content of his journalistic writing differs markedly from that contained in these pages, certain qualities perdure: irony, brevity, the illuminating anecdote, the contempt for rhetoric and bluster.

Indeed, in the appreciations of his work that followed his death, it was the *asciuttezza* of his prose—dryness, literally, but intended here to connote concision, an acute economy of means—that was remarked upon. It was this capacity for synthesis that made possible—as the one-time figurehead of the PCI left Pietro Ingrao noted—Pintor's 'cross between observations of the everyday and the representation of a general kernel'. It also allowed him, as Rossanda put it, 'to nail down the weakness of his adversary with elegance and give the right words to the subalterns who seek to become a general class'.[6] The literary critic and historian Alberto Asor Rosa aptly noted that the truth of Pintor was in his style.[7] More precisely, and with reference to the volumes collected here, Asor Rosa underscores the way in which the effect of Pintor's writing is synthetic, though the syntax is more complex than it at first appears. Even in complexity, however, each component is essential, sparse, and the result that of sculpture, incision, rather than description. It is a style, Asor Rosa observes, in which only some things can be said—the essential ones.

---

6 See Pietro Ingrao, 'Il mio errore' (interview) and Rossana Rossanda, 'Un comunista irreconciliato', *La rivista del manifesto* 41 (July–August 2003). The latter is available at www.larivistadel-manifesto.it/archivio/41/41A20030715.html

7 See Alberto Asor Rosa, 'Il politico e il suo doppio', *La rivista del manifesto* 41 (July–August 2003). Available at www.larivistadel-manifesto.it/archivio/41/41A20030716.html

Here, these are not the cruxes and conjunctures of politics and history, but failure, absence and grief—in particular, the death at war of Giaime and the loss of his Sardinian home, relayed and compounded by the bereavement of his later years. Hence the deep, if dry, desolation in these pages, and the manner in which we perceive the spirit of Giacomo Leopardi—the great poet and aphorist of anti-Romantic pessimism—prevail over that of Marx.

And yet, lest Pintor be drawn into company he would have loathed to keep—those who instrumentalize tragedy and finitude to demean struggles against injustice—we should not forget that the syntax which in these pages works to etch lines of pain and regret was in many ways the same which, over the same years, worked unrelentingly to afflict the comfortable. Perhaps Leopardi and Marx, pessimism and communism, are not incompatible in the end.[8] So much is suggested by the note with which Pintor introduced one of his collections of editorials, *Parole al vento* (Words in the Wind): 'Of one thing I am in any case sure, of what readers will *not* find here—a single line that shows indulgence towards the arrogance that surrounds us and insensitivity to the fate of those who suffer it. The word communism is not so mysterious after all, if this is what inspires it. It is perhaps the most noble of words in the wind.'

Alberto Toscano
2012

---

8 This was the gambit of an Italian contemporary of Pintor's, Sebastiano Timpanaro. See his *On Materialism* (Lawrence Garner trans., London: Verso, 1985).

Servabo

A Fin de siècle *Memoir*

*The most useful books are those of which readers themselves
compose half; they extend the thoughts of which the germ is
presented to them; they correct what seems defective to them,
and they fortify by their reflections what seems to them weak.*

Voltaire

Prologue

I

In his message from beyond the grave, which I'd prefer not to have received, my brother recounts how the war showed him the world in a different light and sealed his fate. Without the war, he'd have remained a writer. Travel and friendships, an instinct for imagination or meeting a girl, would have mattered more than any party or doctrine. He would have continued to believe in individual experience, the history of one man alone, and wouldn't have sacrificed his prerogatives to a collective faith.

He was twenty years old, but his life was perfectly defined and his future readily imaginable. His manuscripts in tiny handwriting fill two chests; I don't know how he did so much in so short a space of time. The war intervened, destroying this orderly existence and prompting him to desperate action.

When he wrote that message he felt death close at hand. It arrived three days later and, when I read it, it didn't strike me because it called for revolution but because of how his youth was vanishing. I don't know anyone who built himself up, and then cut himself down, with such speed.

I fear he was wrong to underplay his death with the argument that no one is irreplaceable (today, I'm forty years older and can contradict him—he's the younger brother). Had he lived, he'd have encountered the same dilemmas as us but could have perhaps come up with better answers.

Without the war, I myself can't say how I'd have grown up and what I'd have done. As a boy, I had no particular bent, not even a facility, for learning. I felt as comfortable on a bicycle or with a ball in the open air as I was ill at ease with multiplication tables behind my school desk. I can only fantasize about the road I'd have taken, like someone who for fun imagines being born again in a different century and taking to sea in a sailing ship.

Perhaps I'd have filled my time with music, in line with the wishes of my father, who wrongly attributed to me his own temperament and gifts I didn't possess (music is a delicate art, difficult to approach); or maybe with film, magical and astounding adventure of our childhood. But I like to think I'd have preferred these imaginary worlds to the real one and that, had it not been for the war, politics would have remained a secondary interest for me too.

But I was fourteen when the war began and twenty when it ended, so that it was superimposed on my adolescence with the precision of a decal. It spared me and I can't even say I fought in it, other than marginally. But in those few years, in an extremely rapid sequence of events, I saw the whole world with which I was familiar—the one

I'd known as a child and which was still living in me—
shattered to pieces.

Many people of all ages went through the war and
remained marked by it (obviously, I'm referring to the
survivors). But they confine it to a different time, like an
almost unreal experience that has nothing to do with the
normality of existence. Not for me—those events
completely determined my future, forming my whole way
of thinking and behaving.

Without the war, my character would certainly have
kept me far removed from public life. I didn't want to
become king or pope; I didn't have the childish need to
excel and dominate others that fuels political ambition in
adults, often to excess. Out of a spirit of contradiction I
preferred the losers, angrily siding with the redskins and
Ethiopians against the conquering, plundering races; and
when the neighbourhood poor trooped to the house door,
for Friday alms, I was sad. But I doubt whether I can deduce
a revolutionary disposition from these noble sentiments.

Similarly, without the war my private life would have
been less burdened with the duties and misunderstandings
that have accompanied it. For example, I don't think I'd have
thrown myself into the adventure of fatherhood so prematurely if I hadn't sought redress or reparation, out of a
desire to reconstruct, as if by a miracle, the emotional
world destroyed by the war. I'd have taken things more
slowly and indulged more in the need for gaiety we all share.

It would be foolish of me to attribute everything good
or bad that has happened to me to external factors. It's likely
that, owing to a character defect or congenital weakness, I

was more prone, from the very beginning, to suffer the legacy of the war. When I was very young, an inscription under the portrait of an ancestor struck me, a mysterious Latin word: *servabo*. It can mean: I will conserve, I will hold in reserve, I will keep faith, or I will serve, I will be useful. But to conserve or to serve are unbecoming terms—they imply subjection, the sense of a limit, a bond. So it may be that if my psychology has remained a prisoner of the war and other adverse events, it's all the fault of that ancestor and his enigmatic precept.

The Island

II

I was ill prepared by a family setting that was informal and protective and that didn't leave room for nasty surprises. I was troubled at heart, liable to childish upsets, and had a recurrent dream about an old woman who tied me in a sack amid the indifference of passers-by. But I have every reason to believe that adolescence would have been as benign for me as childhood. The rumble of thunder heard in the distance was no concern of mine; I still couldn't tell apart a seventeenth-century charge on a cinema screen and Polish cavalry clashing with German tanks in an illustrated newspaper.

We lived on the remote island of the Sardinians, at a time when travelling to and from the mainland was quite an undertaking. The steamer seemed to cross an ocean and the rare hydroplanes fired the imagination. Astonished, from the balconies of the house I saw them take off from the marshes or land in a spray of foam as in the South Sea Islands, discovered at the cinema or in adventure stories.

I experienced no restrictions. For us the city was a playground, its old quarter perched on a rock, its ramparts and towers, its alleyways, sloping towards the port like rivulets, afforded us unlimited physical freedom. It was an extraordinary piece of good fortune that I'll never stop looking back on with regret, especially when I compare it with the prisons of modernity.

Immediately beyond this domain we encountered the countryside in fast bike rides, dusty roads, the white expanse of the salt deposits, and the big windy beaches, to which we migrated en masse in summer on little trains that recalled those of the wild west. An intensive season of swimming began on the last day of school and ended with the autumn storms. I've calculated that I spent at least a thousand festive days on those African beaches, 'in and out of the water like riverside animals',* without any rule other than the one laid down by the path of the sun. More than in the memory, these hours remain imprinted on the body, like a bundle of unalterable sensations that a morning's light and a gust of wind can summon up without warning.

From my brother I learnt games that revealed the secrets of imagination and organization; from his nighttime stories the deeds of paladins, the tricks of the Achaeans, the raids of the black corsair** and the tangled plots of melodramas. From the poorest children of the neighbourhood, who played barefoot with balls fashioned out of rags and could accurately hit any target with stones, I learnt dexterity and a taste for anarchy. I was ready to

---

* The phrase is from Pintor's brother Giaime.

** *Il Corsaro Nero* was a very popular adventure novel by Emilio Salgari published in 1898, the first in a series of five.

succumb to any temptation and in the dark of three picture houses, whose every secret I knew, I experienced emotions that the big stages and little screens of the future would prove incapable of matching.

No bad omen menaced this landscape or my domestic calm. Strange and much loved was our house, perched as if by chance between rocks and caper bushes, high and solitary overlooking the city, with its garden suspended in the air and the mirror of the sea and marshes beyond the roofs of the suburbs, in the circle of the hills. Every hour of the day the sun filtered through the shutters, turning the floors red, and the wind slammed the doors shut, whistling down the corridors.

Family life was gentle and without frills. We kept ourselves warm in winter with a single charcoal burner; we bathed in a zinc bath with pots of boiling water and the air tempered with a fire; we ate large quantities of toasted bread; and we had exclusive use of a large bare room where we were allowed to do anything. Busy with other things, that was how our parents guarded their intimacy and ours.

In the evening, crouched on an uncomfortable straw armchair, my father operated a massive radio and listened to music from every part of the world, while my mother, at a nearby table, corrected school work or wrote countless letters. The house was full of sounds. In summer they entered from the open windows and in winter they bounced off the misted window panes; and I went to sleep listening to them.

Perhaps they—my parents—were not so at peace, regretted the lost opportunities of youth passed in big cities and felt the future was uncertain. But I was unaware of these problems. At times, in the evening, they feverishly transcribed office papers, but talking about money in the family was strictly forbidden. For having done so, I received one of the few slaps of my life.

I couldn't imagine that such a peaceful house would be swallowed up by the earth as if a spell had been cast on it. In its place, there is now a rocky spur where a plaque is fixed referring to my brother, who grew up there between invisible walls. If someone enters this bend and casually reads the inscription, they will be put in mind of a follower of Garibaldi, a trench in the Karst, or civil war. And, indeed, there's no difference.

The City

III

It was a historic June day. The nation went noisily to war, I miraculously passed my *ginnasio* exam* and the family fled the happy island for good. My father was convinced we'd be bombed from all sides, that the island would be invaded and that we'd be cut off from the rest of the world. He was extremely agitated and had no peace until he saw us on the bridge of the steamer, my mother, my sisters and me.

I performed the farewell rites, though I didn't at all envisage a permanent departure. I went to say goodbye to the beaches, where a furious wind blew that day and the waves swept over the coloured wood cabins, forming great pools of foam on the sand. In tears I embraced my beloved aunts and cousins, who'd raised me with great generosity and who would have continued to pray for me with their

---

* In the Italian school system, the *ginnasio* covers the first two years of the *liceo classico*, the branch of high-school education focussed on the teaching of humanities, and emphasizing the study of letters, history, Greek, Latin and philosophy.

mother-of-pearl rosaries. I took leave of my literature teacher, who was fond of me and to whom I owed my success in the exams. And under the almond tree in the garden, my great playmate, I buried a treasure box I never found again.

Even so, on leaving the port, I gazed from the steamer with the typical ingratitude of youth on the facade of the house, which shrank along with the familiar landscape, the avenues on which I'd ridden my bike, the parade grounds of our football games and the ramparts of my first romantic encounters. For me that journey was an opportunity full of promise and it cheered me more than it disturbed me.

Awaiting me were the cobbles of the capital, the solemn cupolas against the sky, the tidy gardens and sumptuous fountains that had amazed me on short holidays, the din and odours of modernity, the articulated trams which circled the city, the lifts and telephones with many numbers, a hundred and two cinemas that my brother had counted for me, new friendships and less imaginary girls than the girlfriends I'd left behind on the island. And also studies more attuned to the virtuoso world of my paternal aunt and uncle. In their hospitable home, which smelt of books and polish, I was to learn many things and get to know a different humanity.

This sunny prospect was clouded at a stroke, like a stormy sky. It wasn't the war, which barely unsettled the city with the whistling of air-raid sirens, but two bereavements that struck my family life simultaneously, unbalancing everything, as if an evil spell had hung over our emigration and opened the gates to hostile forces.

A malaise whose nature wasn't clear to anyone carried off my father, who was saddened in his last days by the thought that he hadn't reached pensionable age. Shortly before, one of his brothers, the severe uncle who was a general, had died in a military plane crash in obscure circumstances. His funeral stunned me by its solemnity. Behind the empty coffin, military bands played funeral marches between squadrons on horseback, armoured vehicles and the insignia of all branches of the military. And it seemed to me a terrible injustice that there was no music at my father's funeral.

Highly sympathetic, the teacher at my high school told me that to lose a father at fifteen is sadder and more dangerous than one imagines. And my brother, who was now also my father, warned me against melancholy. The calm confidence he conveyed, his aversion to those outpourings of the romantic soul that he translated so well into poetry, were a habit with which he protected himself.

As though I'd contracted a debt, in the wake of these events I resumed with devotion the musical studies I'd been initiated into as a child. I went to lessons in the evening, taking the last tram back home or crossing the silent city on foot. With my teacher I worked out a rigid five-year plan that intertwined piano exams and composition with my university examinations, and I even ruled out unduly demanding romances. But I was irremediably behind and I knew I would never master that black-and-white keyboard. In the air and in my soul, round me and within me, I felt a great precariousness, well before the war arrived on the streets and swept away the last vestiges of the past.

IV

When the war entered the city, I was still incredulous. It entered furtively, with bursts of gunfire in the suburbs and the odd desperate clash, surprising unarmed, frightened people. In those days of utter confusion, accompanying my brother through ministries and barracks and following him on improvised demonstrations, I'd seen every attempt to organize armed defence fail. But the illusion that the occupation would only be a brief parenthesis was widespread. And when he left for the south on makeshift transport, with ambitious plans for counter-attack, I had no doubt we'd meet again in peace after a few weeks.

For a time I was caught up in a series of minor adventures, in a climate of conspiracy I didn't take seriously. To avoid the conscription notices, I ended up in a house in the country where I played chess and in a convent where *gerarchi** wandered about disguised as priests. But I soon returned to the streets because the risk was modest and preferable to humiliation. Even during

---

* Members of the National Fascist Party, literally 'hierarchs'.

curfew hours I began to venture out of the house, to hang little red flags on trees and lamp posts. These were the flags that had vanquished the German armies on the battlefield and disgraced their crooked crosses, the flags on which the honour of the world depended at that time. I shall never understand how many who lived through such a great moment have forgotten it to the point of inverting its meaning.

If, one Sunday afternoon, I began to fire at strangers in the middle of a street, I can't say to what extent it was a conscious choice or force of circumstance. I wasn't a fearful child, but I wasn't unduly brave either. I had no inclination to violence and had never even handled an air-gun. How I came to undertake this action is a question to which I've given many different answers over the years, none of them conclusive.

I wasn't alone; the five of us were schoolmates. I'd been at a concert, gripping a pistol and a small hand grenade—the sum total of our arsenal—in my pockets. Outside the theatre we came across two soldiers and followed them for a long time, without deciding on anything. Finally, at the exit of a public park, we quickly caught up with them and fired. My weapon was so covered in sweat it jammed, leaving me dazed.

I fled in haste, losing my hat. I'd never worn a hat—it was a childish disguise—and for no apparent reason went back to retrieve it. Some people had gotten off a tram and begun to yell and chase us; maybe our undertaking looked more like a hold-up than a military action. But I ran quickly, I had the little bomb in my hand, the pursuers dispersed and we made off down side roads.

I could offer many explanations; the simplest is that we were in a war. Others like me had been fighting it for some time, an invisible and therefore more treacherous war, filtering into everyday life, punctuated by ambushes, in a grey city where it seemed to me it was always raining.

Around that time, many unarmed people had been massacred in caves outside the city. I can confirm that, like all invading forces, the German police were hateful, but with an additional characteristic—racial pride and that innate taste for orders which (as someone has said) is the worst of human instincts. This is something difficult to understand if you haven't experienced it, but those grey uniforms, those pointed weapons, those raucous yells, that sheer cruelty, forced the mildest of people to rebel.

I'd learnt that my brother was dead; the news had reached me with incredible violence and this too might explain my conduct. But I don't think so. In my memories, there's no feeling of revenge or retaliation; the blow I'd received was more than skin-deep.

If anything, it was out of a sense of duty, which can be deceptive if not accompanied by mature conviction. Or maybe it was simply a question of circumstances. In the end it's always a question of circumstances. But I'd like to think that no circumstances will again make me act as I did that afternoon, against a chance target, even if I were to be the same age.

The Landmine

·

V

I don't know why the person entrusted with the infor-
mation didn't speak to me about it calmly in his house. He
summoned me like a conspirator to the basement of an
aristocratic building, cluttered with trunks and camp beds,
which served as a night shelter. And in that unreal
atmosphere, by the feeble light of a lamp, he began an
absurd tale.

A small group, a December night, a remote village in
the south, a frontline to cross, a country path beside a
stream, a mined field missed by the pathfinders, a firefight,
an explosion in the dark. And in the first light of dawn the
body lying prostrate in a vineyard under a wall.

It was an idiotic sequence of words that didn't in the
least correspond to my brother's image. Anyone who knew
him like I did couldn't recognize him all of a sudden as so
vulnerable, in that spot like something out of a novel, in
that unnatural position, deaf to any call, inert in the day
and the night under a winter sky. Even after many years,
I've never been able to take in such an implausible scenario.

Weird, confused thoughts possessed me. Perhaps in those September days, when I'd set off on bike on the consular roads* to look for a gap between the roadblocks, I could have told him that the city was surrounded and dissuaded him from his plans. Or I too might have been on that mission and suggested to him that he seek shelter in a ditch rather than a vineyard. These were strange thoughts bound up with our games, bike races and duels with peashooters in the garden, stratagems to abolish time.

The tale continued with many details—that the English were involved, that there was a map drawn by a survivor, that there was a letter for me somewhere, that the life of others parachuted in behind the lines depended on it and that therefore it was necessary to keep the news secret. So a lot of time had passed and I'd been kept in the dark; who knows what had become of that unburied body.

I left that basement a little after dawn; the streets were colder than usual and I didn't encounter anyone. I remember the city as always being rainy, but that February morning it rained in earnest. I got home drenched, with a fixed thought—how can I tell my mother? She was a wise woman, but this death, coming on top of her husband's, was too much.

In peacetime it wouldn't prove easy to reach that crumbling village, that gully and that vineyard which had been described to me in such minute detail. With my old uncle, dejected and silent, I travelled for several

---

* The *vie* or *strade consolari* were the main transport arteries built in ancient Rome to facilitate the movement of troops or goods. Among them are the Via Appia, the Via Cassia and the Via Salaria.

days, passing through bleak villages in a landscape where age-old poverty was compounded by devastation. When war recedes, its traces are ghostly; there were improvised cemeteries and villages where no wall above a metre in height remained standing. Having arrived at our destination, we didn't find a single burial mound where we'd expected it, but more than one—the corpses of soldiers of various nationalities and unfortunate civilians.

It was a highly unusual funeral service. Without the aid of an impromptu gravedigger, we wouldn't even have approximately identified the remains of that strange person who had galoshes in his knapsack because he didn't like the discomforts of bad weather. Not only a violent death, but, judging from the broken vertebrae, an abrupt one. Bent over the grave, my old uncle, *sapiens cor et intelligibile*,* carried out the formal identification.

I wasn't used to this and perhaps I should have let the dead bury the dead, as recommended by his message from beyond the grave. But the local peasants, women in mourning and barefoot children honoured with waving flags this exhumation and the transfer of the body to a less irregular grave. For me this was melancholy confirmation, among so many furnished by the war, of those popular virtues that will remain an indestructible myth of my youth.

---

* 'A wise heart, and which hath understanding', Ecclesiastes 3:32.

Prison

VII

I managed to end up in prison one May evening, shortly before peace arrived. We were caught as a result of conspiratorial carelessness, my closest friend and me, on the eve of a suicide mission I'll recount some other time. Only our young associate in the escapade, likewise careless but with greater talent, escaped arrest by lowering herself onto the rooftops in the middle of the night.

I'd stayed at home so as not to miss out on a white-flour focaccia. The men who came to take me away thought for a moment they'd made a mistake; this genteel house didn't chime with their image of the subversive. But they took the opportunity to snatch my father's pocket watch and other things they reckoned of value. It was a famous gang of irregulars, who had rampaged for months through the city with the help of an informer, the very gang we had wanted to smash.

They took me off to their headquarters, a guesthouse with a garden, full of mirrors and crystal lamps, run by a terror-stricken Neapolitan. I'd been blindfolded and couldn't figure out where I'd ended up. It was like an artificial set straight out of a film.

Their leader was a young cavalry lieutenant, an Italian with a foreign name who acted his part with ostentation. They sat me down on a stool in front of his table, and ten or so of them formed a circle round me and for many hours, in successive waves, laid into me with some cruelty. In the intervals, the young lieutenant made himself scrambled eggs.

They suspected me of being behind an attack on their base and hammered away to get to the bottom of it. I hadn't expected this kind of treatment and it scared me. But at that age one's good at taking it and simulating; and hatred of the violence inflicted provides excellent succour. And then there was something in my appearance and social condition they found disconcerting. And when they threatened to shoot me in the garden, simulating an attempt at escape, I realized they weren't capable of it.

They finally shut me in a little toilet with a very wary old bricklayer. He had swollen limbs and cursed without addressing his words to me. I must have seemed too young and educated to warrant trust, even though I'd been beaten up like him. But then his mood changed and on the second day he encouraged me with great kindness. For me it was a lesson I haven't forgotten and from which I learnt, before reading it in books, that the workers would free the world by freeing themselves.

I was anxious to know what fate had befallen my friend. When I met him in another kind of cell—a coal hole—he had two broken ribs and was losing blood. But he retained his vaguely sardonic air, that annoyance of his at the way of the world. We were mortified at having fallen into a trap that also endangered others. But basically we'd done our best and now, finding ourselves together again, we cheered up.

The last day of May found us once more in that coal hole, us two alone, after a period of respite in the city jails full of bedbugs but also of good bread. In this solitude, sitting on piles of coal, we understood that things were looking very bad for us. Finally, a guard came down to tell us he'd just killed a friend of ours in the street and that we would be shot the following day. News of the imminent execution spread through the city and we were being mourned as dead. One of my sisters prayed for me with a future pope.

By contrast, we felt curiously relieved, because—we weren't going to end up in German hands. The idea of having to face scientific torture terrified us more than anything else. Death, on the other hand, is very difficult to grasp at that age. We weren't able to imagine ourselves blindfolded in the courtyard of a barracks, or tied to a chair in a meadow on the outskirts, or shot in the back of the neck in a cave. The whole night long we spoke of other matters and of none.

Only in the early morning were we distracted by the shuffling of rare passers-by on a pavement grate above our heads. This was our neighbourhood; a hundred metres away was our school; maybe these invisible passers-by were people we knew; and we abandoned ourselves to melancholy thoughts. Above all, I thought about how I was doing my mother a great wrong, dying as I was in the wake of my father and brother—a veritable massacre.

Another member of the gang came in without saying a word, escorted us through staircases and deserted corridors, loaded us onto a requisitioned taxi, and deposited us, incredulous, at the city jails. Artillery fire could be heard, the Americans were at the city gates, and we hadn't survived by a miracle but as a result of timetabling.

Three days later, we emerged into the sunshine, free. Germans in camouflage fatigues on muddy tanks were still making their way up the riverbank. At home they weren't expecting us; they thought that we were alive but had been deported to the north. For my friend that would have been very fortunate; he wouldn't have died obstinately on a different battle front, hit by shrapnel, a few days before the armistice, buried with an absurd helmet on his grave. He might be called a hero, but I prefer to remember him as a heedless lad.

Peace

VII

The last bomb, awesome invention of the century, had exploded and in that infernal blaze the war ended. It was time to celebrate, to make up for the hardships, to resume one's occupation, to return to normality. And everyone did it with the frenzy that accompanies the novelty of peace, when war is merely a parenthesis to be hastily closed, casting out its last demons. But I no longer had habits and didn't know what pursuits to turn to.

For me, normality meant taking exams in history and philosophy, doing mechanical exercises on the piano, participating in meetings with anthems and flags, flirting in gardens that had turned green again and recovering my good spirits. It meant recognizing that the world turned as it did before, that nothing irreparable had happened, that life reasserted its rights.

But for me the post-war air didn't possess such lightness; I didn't breathe it with such nonchalance, nor did I want to. I felt a sense of foreignness, isolation and suspicion; daily life had lost its old flavour. The exams, the piano practice and the meetings too closely resembled a convenient distraction. It was too disproportionate; too many people had died. That normality looked like desertion.

I wasn't even sure that the war was over. Instead, it seemed like a truce full of threats, as if human beings had learnt nothing and that legacy of corpses and rubble hadn't converted them to wisdom, but trained them for a future hecatomb. The victors were strangely similar to the vanquished, swapping parts and becoming enemies again, as if the war had been emptied of the promises that had ennobled it, and now revealed its true character, the iron rule of an unchanging history.

I was amazed that normality could so rapidly reproduce along with the same habits also the same vices. Now there weren't so many uniforms, everyone put on featureless clothing, but the difference in fates—the division between superiors and inferiors that was so obvious in the war—re-emerged in identical fashion under the guise. Those who once again commanded in the new institutions fit the descriptions of their predecessors; those who once again obeyed in daily life suffered the same humiliations; the strongest and the weakest played the same roles without variations.

A strange and sudden metamorphosis took place—people's gazes no longer carried that demand and that offer of solidarity which they had silently communicated in the days of suffering. Now a desire for compensation inspired all against all, with everyone in pursuit of their share of the spoils, in the big fair that I was to learn to call capitalist, where misery and abundance and every kind of commodity are ceaselessly bought and sold. And even the new passions of politics, the impassioned speeches, the suggestive powers of leaders and symbols, had a feeble sound compared to the din of war still in the air.

Against this background even the simplest things, the most private and intimate ones, seemed to me faded and slight, scattered and elusive. House, books, objects, domestic conversations, stories and memories—these belonged to a fallen order that could not be restored in any way but demanded to be (who knows how!) reinvented from top to bottom.

At the age of twenty, this is what I told myself without knowing what to do. Too often my thoughts went to that southern village and when I happened to meet my old cellmate, who'd gone back to his trade as a bricklayer, I experienced a vague sense of guilt. I felt that the mobilization proclaimed in the days of iron and fire* couldn't end in banality and I looked round for some task to shoulder. And so it was that I convinced myself to take sides,** not for great endeavours which no one envisioned any more, but to share the company of the less fortunate and defend their good causes.

---

* *Ferro e fuoco* is an expression, taken from the Latin *ferro ignique*, referring to scorched-earth tactics in war.

** The expression used by Pintor is *prendere partito*—literally, to take (a) party.

Marriage

VIII

Like our clandestine escapades, getting married was an innocent impulse. She was the friend who'd escaped over the rooftops and, like me, was twenty. We'd experienced the same risks, lived two steps away from one another in that neighbourhood where we carried out our studies and our private war, and I was tired of courting her under the false pretences required by the customs of the time. She had an oriental face and beautiful eyes with which it was easy to fall in love with, and marriage was the condition for living together more freely, a kind of rapture.

We didn't have money; both of us had modest jobs, without any vocational background or further plans, in that post-war climate of provisionality which makes everything seem easier after the hardships endured. I was less used to poverty than her; she'd always had a difficult life and in the occupied city wore shoes tied with wire laces. We ate dreadful fried food in canteens or small *rosticcerias* or cherries wrapped in paper bags in suburban meadows we reached by tram. The legacy of the war, but extreme youth too, is positive in this respect—one doesn't have (or at least we didn't) the greed that sets in in times of opulence.

A coffee machine and an iron were our most luxurious wedding presents, essential in the room where we first went to live, which belonged to a déclassée widow who ate at the same table as us. It was a major improvement some time later to find a room of our own in the suburbs, above a noisy fish market, extorted from the institutions of the time. A very small room, and a very narrow staircase to reach it. Neither were compatible with a piano.

Even in these youthful moves I dragged my old instrument along, bulky and useless now that our hours were long, we had other problems and our minds were elsewhere. But I wasn't sorry to have lost my privileges, perhaps because I knew that privileges are shelved but never lost. And naturally, when our first son was unexpectedly announced, we began to violate our commitment to the principle of a working-class wage with little subterfuges. We could invoke the extenuating circumstance that another principle of revolutionary morality—the protection of motherhood—was disregarded in the actual conduct of political organizations.

There was optimism in this makeshift existence, which sought to erase bad memories and made do with amusements created from nothing, and in the idea we had of the future of the world. Individual needs weren't disconnected from collective ones in the perception, or illusion, of a shared destiny. If it wasn't optimism—a natural gift neither of us possessed—it was a generous naivety, as if the events of the war hadn't forced us to grow up more quickly and become more sensible, but had fixed us in the ingenuousness of adolescence.

We hadn't imagined ourselves as parents and, when that's what we became, we didn't succeed in feeling like adults at last and behaving accordingly. We had no experience, and we didn't even possess the self-confidence that distinguishes a good parent from a bad one. I missed the free space of my childhood. A sixth floor isn't suitable for children and I was forever afraid they'd fall out of the windows. For her it was the start of the problems that complicate the life and work of women more than those of men.

This is a difficult and delicate issue. I can't now know what memory she'd have, were she still alive, of those early years and the ones that followed and which ended very unhappily. For my part I can say that I reacted to the inexperience with the devoted, anxious attitude which can be generated by strong feelings, but which soon becomes undue interference and doesn't help others to grow in accordance with their own nature.

The Trade

IX

It was only a newspaper but for us it was much more than that, and joining it wasn't a career choice but a form of voluntary enlistment. It was said that, for some people, prison had been their university, forming combatants of a special cast. A paper was much more comfortable than a prison, but it could have the same function, being experienced too as a training camp, a community and a school, a border where the state of emergency is, by definition, an everyday affair.

But I'd retained what I had heard—revolutions succeed when they are prepared by those, the poets and painters, who have nothing to do with them, but only as long as they know what part they're supposed to play. And because workers on their own can make a whole host of things better than anyone else, but most likely not an immaterial product like a paper, I was persuaded that this was a task for the educated young, as long as they shouldered it as a special task, a task of honour.

I was an excellent subordinate—we all were—and we volunteered for any job according to a criterion of communal utility. In that apprenticeship, it wasn't disappointing to realize that scruples were more highly appreciated than initiative, uniformity than creativity. A maxim of the time stated that from small beginnings come great things— there was even a sign with this inscription hung on a wall—and that seemed to us satisfaction enough. A brave old fighter reminded us to switch off the lights when they weren't needed, because that was the workers' money.

We were welcome in the arena, the youngest ones like me, because we conformed to rules and standards set elsewhere, in legendary places and by experienced men who came from afar and deserved reverence; we considered it due and didn't in the least resent it. We willingly rendered our tribute to these severe masters, unquestioned repositories of a collective faith. To depart in our ideas and behaviour from the boundaries set for us meant embarking on the slippery slope of worldly enticements. Many of us, after all, came from a social class that was naturally exposed to such enticements.

This rule applied not only to important things, but also to very minor ones. To go to the cinema rather than meetings in the suburbs or put aside cash for a family holiday—these were furtive acts. If for us a worker's wage was the correct standard, and the precondition for maintaining a universal point of view, it was a misdeed to supplement it with any tricks. If we worked without personal profit or ambition, as if bound by a vow, it was reprehensible to seek compensation elsewhere, even in casual romances.

In this collegiate existence there was room for a spirit of friendship, a sense of steering the future, and, hence, also excitement and fun. We worked very late, until five in the morning, but the work performed repaid the exertion. Outside the print works, where milk was still drunk to guard against lead poisoning, there was a pastry shop in an alleyway where piping-hot fritters rolled on a strip of sugar. A collective van equipped with benches, like those in public service in the post-war days, made a tour of the city at dawn to carry us off to bed. And in that enclosed space were born forbidden loves, but also legitimate marriages, rejuvenating the community.

The idea of confronting enemy propaganda on our own was a source of pride and a goad to hone our skills. For years I applied to writing the meticulous techniques employed on a piano keyboard. I cut and polished my texts printed in the paper, endless accounts of speeches by others and timid personal efforts, discovering that there's always one line too many out of every three and reaching the conclusion that (as I still maintain) two pages are enough to exhaust any subject.

I now think I practispractised a trade and a kind of existence very different from the ones I envisaged. Two pages daily accumulated over the years, like the Colombian golden fish in the novel,* form a pile twelve thousand calendar sheets high, a long stretch of life. But I didn't doubt it was worth the trouble then, because people of good will (plain and simple people,** as we preferred to put it) would change the world.

---

* A reference to Gabriel García Marquéz's *One Hundred Years of Solitude*.

** *gli uomini semplici*

The Scene

X

Just as one gazes at the sky from an astronomical observatory, I looked out from my post on a great scene and thought I was participating in the motion of the stars while I sat at a typewriter. It was a time when passions clouded the critical spirit and passivity was sometimes confused with action. But they were genuine passions, nobly inscribed in the gigantic frame of history, the clash of opposed civilizations, the irreducible conflict between classes.

It was simple and just to take a side. One day, by improvised transport, I reached a spot in the countryside where two farmhands had died a few hours earlier, killed by police gunfire, with a brutality frequent at the time. In a room similar to a whitewashed grotto, the bodies were watched over by grieving women, wrapped in black shawls like my Sardinian aunts and cousins. For me, there was no difference between this spectacle and the still-living memory of the war; no difference between the high-up culprits of this rural crime and the philosophy of privilege that had set the world on fire. It wasn't an episode but a symbol. There are two worlds—these dead men belonged to the worthier one and they were my brothers.

It was right to take a side even when it wasn't so simple. I made another trip, to the legendary east where the lower orders, soldiers and workers, had triumphed in their revolution for the first time in millennia. More so than by other bad signs, which I put down to the harshness of history, I was struck by the prostitutes warming themselves by fires in the streets of these cities, as they did in our suburbs. It didn't amaze me that people had remained in poverty, but that they had forgotten fraternity. I would never stop thinking there are two worlds, but I would come to learn that the dividing line is not marked on any atlas and even runs through the human heart. Taking a side would become more complicated, but more necessary.

It was right to take sides even where the dividing-line thins to vanishing point, in the cold institutions where power celebrates itself, auditoria and sumptuous palaces where steps go round in circles along blind routes, images chase one another in a game of mirrors, speech is muffled, and thoughts brush the truth aside. Here, where my daily work brought me, it was easy to go astray; here, the two worlds blur into the worse one and taking sides is an oath to be repeated every day.

Very belatedly, I understood that our lenses were weak and our instruments antiquated; and that observing a great scene does not mean understanding it, still less influencing it—just like getting stirred up about an electoral contest is not equivalent to storming the Bastille. And even more slowly I realized the scene had changed round me, in tandem with my age, in an utterly unforeseen way.

In the space of a quarter-century, the language of the people, the sound of the streets, the value of things, the mood of the young, the gait of women—all these had changed, not only in the great continents but also in the next room, in the privacy of one's home. Everything had changed except the one thing that determines every other—enmity as the spirit of the world.

XI

The first time I had to step up to a microphone, to commemorate my prison comrade, my legs trembled and I left without saying a word. Now that I was older and had a position in the hierarchy, I'd learnt the art of platform oratory in closed rooms or large theatres. But I hadn't understood that this art is unwelcome if it doesn't respect the conventions, and if it crosses a forbidden threshold beyond which any thinking is unauthorized.

I wasn't clad in shining armour and didn't have a marshal's baton in my knapsack. I simply wanted to attend to the warning signals that were arriving from the four points of the compass, to rekindle a lost sensitivity, to rediscover the course that had united us in the distant past. I'd read in revolutionary primers that, in the event of a calamity, everyone should do their best and take responsibility for the whole detachment they belong to, as happens in a hive to each of its guests. This was the spirit— a zealous one—that prompted me to protest.

I didn't anticipate meeting with hostility from audiences, censorship from the party machine, reproach from my superiors, and the prescribed sanctions. I didn't imagine that the harsh teachers of yesteryear were so protective of themselves, so used to equating themselves with what was true and right, that they had lost the capacity either to teach or to learn. I didn't suspect that the same nettles had grown in our enclosures as the ones we wanted to uproot in those of others. I was quite amazed by it and still am.

But, above all, I didn't anticipate (how could I?) returning after what seemed a hundred years to the happy island in such comic circumstances and for such incongruous reasons. I didn't return out of nostalgia, but to submit to an order, to respect discipline and to do penance. I didn't return to rediscover the treasure hidden under the almond tree, but to subject myself to a test. I didn't return voluntarily, but because the machinery I'd lived in so long had broken down with a crash.

With these strange thoughts, and as if in a dream, from the bridge of the steamer I watched the island emerge from the mist and loom up with its colours, just as I'd seen it fade and vanish when I was a child. It emerged from memory and regained its shape, like an inverted film sequence. It was real again and yet remained a fantasy; the past was stronger than the present and held it in its grip.

Disoriented, stepping onto the jetty and looking at the old quarter, I asked myself if my unanticipated exile might be of some use to someone or something in this land, which, for me, was so ancient. I doubted it, but in any case I'd do good work, meticulous and earnest, as long as it was required of me. And if I succumbed to any weakness, setting off in search of lost time, I'd do it in secret.

I would go to live in a village on the shore where the countryside would resemble the one I remembered, so that they became superimposed on one another. In the morning, going to work, I would read the news between the coloured cabins of the pile-dwellings where the smell of algae was strong; and I'd go back there in the hot hours when the wind got up and changed the colour of the sea. Criss-crossing the countryside, where for centuries between shepherds and cultivators no one knows who was in the right, in order to attend routine meetings, I'd take a detour by the hills where we'd sought refuge on the eve of war. Commemorating a legendary hero, in a cinema with the old seats, with embarrassment I would see my primary-school teacher in the audience. Coming back from impatient youth assemblies, which wanted to make the revolution, I'd see the lamps of our street once again swinging in the night. And taking a plane to rejoin my family for a few days, I would regret that it wasn't a hydroplane.

The Outpost

XII

The old mechanism is in pieces, but the time hasn't come for resignation and capitulation. Order does not as yet reign under the heavens and fires still burn all round, in the lowliest of the world's peripheries and in its unruly metropoles. Whether they will spark a new blaze or are but smouldering, scattered residues is difficult to know, but it is still too early to revoke the state of emergency. What's different is that now it's necessary to stand on one's own two feet.

Thirty years on, I once again find myself working at a newspaper of few means, again resembling a community or school, but this time with its own rules and without harsh masters. This time I'm the involuntary master. I can't say if this is a second youth or a senile romance; the two often coincide. It's certainly a risky repeat perform-ance, with the attractions and disenchantments of any repeat performance. It's fun to dust down the old theatre, refurbish the backstage, trace out the stage set with the old costumes, test the lights and look at the empty seats of the auditorium in anticipation of the audience that might or might not turn up.

As ever, I remain a subordinate in spirit and I'm beginning again, with the same diligence, to pile up the calendar sheets, by the hundreds. As ever, it's an improvised existence, with the same artisanal habits, the same smell of lead and ink, the same disproportionate disputes and the same mistakes, even if it's no longer usual to see in the dawn and less innocent distractions take the place of nocturnal van drives. Any reverence is banned; liberty or licence trespass agreeably into anarchy.

For someone like me, these are days of envy. This generation of sons and daughters takes things in its stride; the girls are all very beautiful; they all wear strange outfits or doze peacefully in the very lecture halls where we trembled. Everyone speaks a primitive language but speak all the time, as we wouldn't have dared to, and are certain they know even what they don't know at all. The workers go round on demonstrations, banging tin drums. Many of the gentlemen who live in luxurious buildings or occupy high positions find themselves held in open contempt. Maybe these are ephemeral victories, but they're ones that the generation of fathers and mothers, with its war and dreams and sorrows, never experienced.

In this community, fortalice of the last revolution, a big Chinese wall poster showed up on the third day against the unwitting master I was. Here at last was someone avenging the subjection of our youth. I knew full well that this spirit of rebellion would soon be dampened, that it would experience the same disappointments we did, that we were wandering in a sunlit catacomb, and that we shouldn't confuse our incense fumes with gunpowder. But I kept this awareness to myself, because it was good for a hundred flowers to bloom.

One drawback of age is to see in advance the mistakes everyone repeats in the relay of generations, in accordance with a law that might be called natural. So it was that I too saw this repeat performance run into the same obstacles—imagination overtaken by formulae that imprison the mind, new intuitions slipping into the old beliefs, friendship turning into competition, and means and ends becoming disconnected, as invariably happens.

And yet this outpost in the desert of the tartars,* erected in compliance with my unknown ancestor's precept, has withstood, almost miraculously, a good deal of stormy weather. It hasn't lowered its banners entirely; it hasn't been ingloriously invaded by weeds and brambles like other proud fortresses that were said to be impregnable. For some it's served as a kind of tiny green island, a charming island. And I sometimes end up thinking that even the many ghosts that crowd my memories have visited it and taken a liking to it.

---

* A reference to Dino Buzzati's eponymous novel.

Grief

XIII

There's nothing to be done and you can't be of any help to her, someone told me. It's a rather base platitude that people think or say when, as a result of seeking the truth among the nebulae and making marks with set squares and compasses, they don't see the simple things in front of their eyes. I'd begun with simple things, and that is how both of us had imagined our life in common, but I'd long ago lost sight of them and now I rediscovered them distorted.

An illness can burst into a house, into the private, confined world of each person, with the same impact as an explosive device that demolishes and burns everything round it; or like a poison that insinuates itself into every fibre. But it's not like death, which marks an end. For example, a prolonged death agony that lasts nine years, some of which might be years of fear and decline, while others are ones of handicap and decay, is a form of life. So you can do anything to be of help as you might in normal conditions, or as you might in politics, if its goal were authentic relations between people.

More than anything else, illness shows that the world is divided in two. It's synonymous with separation and solitude. Kind-hearted people feel sympathy, others feel uneasy, yet others experience nuisance and even irritation. But in these different ways they send the same signal of detachment. They reassure themselves and communicate to the other that illness is an exceptional, foreign condition, like old age, and not a common, shared fate. And it's then that illness, not being recognized as a form of existence, becomes horribly painful and incurable.

Money, relationships, enterprise, knowledge, power relations—in such moments these assume enormous significance. One understands more clearly why, in the course of existence, everyone seeks to accumulate these weapons at all costs, so as to be able to deploy them against the final siege. Searching for a rare medicine, demanding attention, or fitting out a room, or usefully beating out the rhythm of the days and nights, are completely different things for those possessed of these weapons and those bereft of them.

In the post-war period, there was a serum for the ailments of maternity which, although nothing special— it was extracted from pregnant mares—was very hard to find. But that was something which only required application. When, by contrast, people depend on the sophisticated mechanisms of modernity and the problem is one of survival, they end up in a deaf and blind labyrinth, where effort alone is insufficient and hope ridiculous.

Such an illness can't be either accepted or denied; one can neither tell the truth nor lie. The only way of fighting it is not to assign it a finishing line—cure or death—but to live it in the present, to regard the future not as an expiry date but as a succession of days, proclaiming normality and rejecting the exception. The worst obstacle is the bodily suffering that manifests itself everywhere, in a thousand forms. But this suffering is also the only one against which the materiality of science has made progress.

More than anything else, what counts are the everyday things that structure existence and give it continuity. Countless things, which press ever more urgently with the passing of years, months and days. Arranging, planning, distracting, encountering people, places and seasons, and then accompanying and supporting when strength fails and the body retreats into itself. In the whole of a life there is nothing more important than bending down so that another, their arm round your neck, can raise themselves up again.

The stupidity of machines that delay death is worse than the stupidity of machines which claim to lighten it, even though their philosophy is one and the same. A nineteenth-century writer relates how his farm dogs stopped barking, intimating and announcing his father's death by their silence. I would like to be able to say that in the end at least I observed this silence.

There's a parallel between the drifts and deviations of public, collective life and those of private, individual life. Looking back, I see this entanglement and ask myself which of the two aspects is less flattering in my case.

Epilogue

XIV

A book is useful to the person who writes it, rarely to those who read it, which is why libraries are full of useless books. In my case these notes are merely a contrivance for reordering in my imagination things that don't add up in reality.

I've written them at a respectable age, as can readily be inferred from their tone. It's an age at which few resist the temptation to look back out of a desire to restore to things a duration they don't in themselves possess. Indulging in this weakness, what is striking is the incredible brevity of the cycle. It's like a strip of celluloid with a few frames, so short that beginning and end coincide.

In reality, virtually none of what I held dear has remained standing. For example, the war I assigned such great importance to was a fleeting business compared with the tangle of ferocity and futility I see round me, which crowns the century and governs our private existence. And I've preferred not to mention names and places and dates that also possessed great significance for me, so as to avoid them crumbling away like dust in my hands.

In truth, the wheel of history revolves backwards splendidly or turns on itself like a spinning top. Should I conclude from this that enduring passions, noble ideals, generous intentions, struggles and mistakes are a mad fairy tale? Certainly not—they are always the salt of the earth and so it has been even in these decades. But a shower suffices to cleanse the earth and salt dissolves in water.

'I am fairly evenly brown in complexion, with a high forehead of reasonable width, light eyes and eyebrows that are bushy but well-shaped. It would be difficult for me to describe the shape of my nose because, to all appearances, it is neither flat nor aquiline, neither large nor pointed. I only know that it is more on the large side and somewhat too sloped. As to the shape of my face, it is either square or oval, but it would be very difficult for me to say which . . . To speak of my character, I am melancholic, to the point that the last three or four years have seen me laugh three or four times. I am intelligent and have no difficulty saying so, but it is an intelligence ruined by melancholy. Indeed, although I have mastered my language rather well, possess a good memory and am not too confused in ideas, I am always so absorbed in my dark mood that I express what I want to say rather badly.'

Maybe I too should have adopted the meticulous descriptive technique of this seventeenth-century gentleman, furnishing a wealth of detail, given that the overall picture is elusive. I'll do it another time, to recount the same stories in pleasanter fashion; or perhaps to relate not the past but the future, what will happen in the half century that certainly awaits me—as the confident lady to whom I dedicate these pages tells me every day.

Miss Kirchgessner

One can be pessimistic about the times and circumstances, about the fate of a country or a class, but one can't be pessimistic about man.

Anonymous

The Omen (1925)

I

When I came into the world, one September day, there was an inauspicious mishap. It had been decided by the family that I'd be called Piero, in honour of a paternal uncle who was a career soldier. But a second paternal uncle—a colonial civil servant—died of fulminant meningitis and I was baptized Lodovico in his memory. An impartial Pierlodovico, which would have suited everyone and dispelled bad omens, didn't occur to anyone.

The Reverend Sterne, a country gentleman, maintains with sound arguments that names are subdivided into good, bad or neutral, and influence our behaviour rather more than is thought. Some prompt noble undertakings, others wickedness or mediocrity. The newborn have no say in the matter and the name imposed on them accompanies them unremittingly from the cradle to the grave. Not even parliamentarians can revoke it.

It's an engaging theory. It comforts me to think that things would have taken a different turn if I'd been a Piero or Pierlodovico; and that some of my relatives would have met with different fates had they not inherited the strange name of one of their ancestors.

More than seventy years have passed since that baptismal day, during which I've done nothing. This sense of uselessness is the essence of old age, otherwise called senility. It's a condition that fascinates novelists but which I strongly advise against.

Distant things seem clear while nearby ones become blurred, as in an inverted spyglass. Important things turn out to be futile and vice versa. Childhood memories crowd in but recent years are like a clean slate. A zealous caretaker has erased any sign.

My profession as a scrivener makes me think of those houses of cards that children like but which collapse at the trembling of a hand. Better to have been born two centuries earlier and imitate Miss Kirchgessner, afflicted by blindness but a virtuoso on the glass harmonica, delighting aristocratic audiences with her glass instrument throughout her life. Sounds are less misleading than words.

My private life might instead be compared to that of a goldfish in a bowl. But it's an inappropriate comparison. Who can exclude the possibility that a goldfish has a lively imagination and an adventurous existence? I don't believe it's limited to going round and round in its little world, as was the case with me.

My state of mind can't be a pathology of age and nothing more. It must have a practical origin in events and circumstances common to everyone. I have a rather vague memory of these events and circumstances, which seem comic or tragic depending on my mood. So I try to sort things out by setting down these confidences, as if I were chasing clouds seated on a park bench.

I'd like to dedicate them to a much-loved prodigal son, but I don't think he would approve. Every day I repeat in his memory—peace be with you, impractical man, stubborn idealist, terrible specimen in a foreign world. But I get no response and no forgiveness.

Sometimes the echo of a stanza we sang together in play reaches me: 'In this dark tomb / let me lie'. The verses aren't beautiful but the music was written by the greatest of composers.

The Shore

II

At the age of three months I landed on the island of the Moors⋆ borne by the water in a wicker basket. In days of yore that island was a recess of Eden and couldn't be reached by a steamship in the company of one's parents. So I arrived as advised by Holy Scripture and remained there fifteen years until the day of the Flood.

No one has told me anything about this landing but I know the sky was bright, the quay sun-drenched and the light white, as is often the case in the island where the sand has dazzling reflections. It's a lie that newborns don't have memories; there is a corporeal memory that's distinct from the mental one, even if scientists can't accept such a truth.

I've retained a clear and distinct perception of that morning and that landscape, the light and the sound, the rippling of the sea under the mistral, the outline of the towers through the haze. I can summon it up at will and I

⋆ The reference is to Sardinia, from the 'flag of the four moors', which remains the island region's emblem.

use it as a touchstone of any morning. It's an emotion anyone can experience, reviving moments nestled in time.

There's a sentimental memory in addition to the corporeal one. Waiting to receive me on the quay was a soft humming, a telling of interwoven fairy tales that enveloped the basket like a choir. There were figures in the shadows whom I saw with my eyes closed. I couldn't tell them apart but I recognize them nonetheless. They all wore long dresses, shawls and headscarves. I knew they were women, something different from men.

They were messengers of benevolence and bearers of affection. Opening my eyes and starting falteringly to walk, from year to year, I'd recognize them not among the shadows but in everyday gestures. Their humming would combine with the cry of the fishermen and carters and the interwoven tales would become conversations in local dialect. But they will never lose the flavour fixed from the very first day in my sentimental memory.

It was a remote past that offered shelter. When, many years later, I returned, the din of machines, crowded on the jetty like metallic flocks, would meet me. I would not hear the hum of fairy tales or the cries of fishermen and carters; and I would not see the towers through the haze. The present deafens the past and conceals it behind high walls.

Dear Parents

III

I was free like a monkey in a forest in the days when monkeys and forests covered the earth. I envied monkeys and imitated them, climbing the garden tree and swinging by my feet. The branches hung over a ditch and the lady on the top floor begged me not to fall.

I roamed along sun-drenched beaches, windy ramparts and rowdy alleyways. I followed the seasons with the instinct of a seabird. I rode on a big bike, played football with off-duty soldiers, entered into the darkness of the cinema stalked by pederasts.

Honour thy father and thy mother is the most out-of-date of the ten commandments. But I willingly subscribe to it because I owe my parents the levity of that time and can't blame them for anything other than having created me. It's a reproach that can be addressed to all parents without denying them gratitude.

I'm sorry my father died unhappy, before his time. He played merrily at tiddlywinks with me on a floor overrun with counters of every shape and colour, with piles of books as forts and chairs as battlefields. Exposed to the elements, the tiddlywinks twisted, becoming invulnerable, and I owed my supremacy to this guile, comparable to the use of drugs in modern armies.

A month before the illness, he took me to a concert where he wept continuously in silence. I remember the mechanical movement with which he wiped his glasses. Then he told me that this last symphony by the Dutchman Ludwig van (a German Beethoven wasn't acceptable) was the only score that would have made him tremble on the podium.

I still have his 1913 engagement as an assistant choir master in an opera house with a greedy Argentinian company, paid by a gratuity. He interrupted his career to marry and my mother did likewise, sacrificing her literary interests. Romantic marriages should be banned.

I'm sorry my mother grew old in the silence of deafness. Why on earth, she asked, do the blind elicit sympathy and the deaf mockery? I remember her in her youth, bent over her table, busy writing tales for children and countless letters to relatives or correcting school work, the square nibs that scraped the sheets. The stroke of the pen bewitched me.

She also wrote my homework, getting the highest marks, and gave me advice I still follow—if you've got to write about Saint Francis, and know nothing about him, talk about the nature surrounding him which you know too, about the trees and hills, wolves and birds, the sun and the moon, water and fire. It's much easier and more appropriate than a theological dispute.

To the light of the island she preferred the shade of the Tuscan hills where she'd grown up and which she missed. But she taught willingly and wrote an anthem for the school—O, botany, zoology!—which an old pupil sent me through the post yesterday.

Aladdin

IV

I'd ask Aladdin's lamp to let me spend a day and a night in the demolished house, reassembling it as it was in those years. My curiosity is so strong that I have sought to persuade a professional to replace the magic lamp by sketching out my memory. I had to make do with an aerial photograph in which a garden and a well are visible.

I don't actually mean the material reality of the house overhanging the city, or the landscape one can still make out, or the wind that banged the door and which I can feel when I close my eyes. I mean an atmosphere I cannot convey in words. Even sorcery might not be enough, because that air was timeless, unadorned and faint, with the smell of coal and the kitchen range.

It was plainness, the moral complement of physical freedom, the opposite of the opulence that imprisons the imagination. I deplore de Tocqueville, who judged the redskins to be without ambition because they desired nothing but a weapon for hunting, a blanket against the cold and an open sky. He didn't understand that simplicity is an immense ambition and the essence of freedom.

Should Aladdin's afternoon be rainy and militate against adventures in the open air, I will dedicate forty minutes to a game of buttons inside the house. I trust in the patience of those listening to me while I explain the workings of this game, which imitated soccer techniques without mechanical props and had the waxed dining-room table as its stadium.

We had eight teams that reproduced the national championship, with first and second rounds and an updated league table. Elaborate rules and penalties prevented a shooting gallery and the result was never 5–0 as in some comic finals. Unintentional ink stains on the table marked out the borders of the playing field and penalty area.

The secret lay in the shape of the buttons, in their grip on the table surface, in their stability or mobility with respect to the roles of forward or defender, in the pressure put on the back of the players by a chip that set them in motion. In particular, the secret lay in the selection, in the discovery of the attitudes of each champion on the wooden benches of the haberdashery, in the cautious pillage of domestic buttons.

My elder brother's favourite squad was composed of concave mother-of-pearl buttons that glided fast, sweeping the ball—a tiny leather button rarely found on sale in shops—along with them. My strongest line-up comprised hefty players made of green glass, who preferred placement and long passes to goalmouth engagement. On

Sundays, the radio broadcast live commentary on the games; the yelling of the fans invaded the room and by magic our table became a turf full of famous champions.

The Cousin

V

I'm not being honest when I paint those far-off years in the colours of the sun and sea and associate them with the wind. That was the physical joy of my age. But the night was lying in wait even before the Flood; and my dreams were inhabited by witches who carried me off.

One of those nights I was bathed in sweat when my father awoke me. I hadn't called him, as often happened, and he wasn't wearing his long white nightshirt but his everyday grey suit. He told me to get dressed and guided me in the dark, under a starry sky, along the road that led to the door and home of our aunts and cousins.

There, dying, was the youngest of our cousins, whose name was Maria as I later read with surprise on her tomb, but who as a child, like everyone else, I called Ninì. She was gasping in bed, with her hair—which she usually wore gathered at the neck—loose, surrounded by the tears and prayers of relatives who thronged the room as on Christmas Day. She pulled me close and asked me breathlessly these three questions: Will Ninì die, will Ninì die, will Ninì die? In her eyes I was a blond, miraculous angel and I signalled no with my head three times.

She died a few hours later; I hadn't cured her and was orphaned of my second mother. My father came to tell me while I was manoeuvring a fleet of bottles in a hollow at the bottom of the garden. I didn't cry at all and went on playing, feeling I was very wicked at heart. I don't know if it was true, or if I was suppressing death.

To deliver me from evil, as the prayer goes, she left me the small sacred medal she wore round her neck. It soon got lost in the sea and once again I was sure I was wicked at heart. They had told me that the good cousin watched over me from on high but perhaps she wouldn't have forgiven my ingratitude this time.

Every Thursday, going to lunch with her sisters, in accordance with a scrupulous ritual, I feared being found out. I wore the little chain under my vest in the hope that my mother would sooner or later come to know what image of paradise was engraved on the medal. But the sacred image lost for ever remained mysterious for ever.

This was my first encounter with the other world and it can't have been an indifferent one if I remember it with a precision unusual in an absent-minded person. There was a style in those bygone deaths, replete with domestic tenderness, deaths which don't take place any more and even then did not fall to everyone.

The Lie

VI

Only now do I realize, to my surprise, that I had a parallel Catholic education. I went to the eleven o'clock Mass, had catechism lessons with a chubby priest, confessed my sins unwillingly once a month (false witness and impure acts) and regularly took part in the Mayday procession in honour of a saint called Ephysius.

These rites weren't practised by my parents. I wasn't obliged to pray in the evening and there were no holy images in the house. But they were popular rites in the city, at school and among relatives, and religious feast days punctuated the year like country fairs and occasions not to be missed.

This custom explains the *nom de guerre* I adopted, in unwitting imitation of the Bolshevik leaders, to confront my imaginary enemies. I was Patì Sottoponzio Pilato,* a Roman consul, commonly called Patì. So often had I heard

---

* Literally, 'Suffered Underpontius Pilate'—a transliteration of a phrase from the Nicene Creed.

those four words, which remained imprinted in me like a jingle, recited in prayer.

This custom might also explain the sense of guilt that tormented me and was to go on tormenting me over the years, like a congenital illness. I suspected I was the epitome of vice and feared tremendous punishments, even though I'd never suffered any. This was why in winter, returning to the house in the dark, I crossed the main entrance in great haste and rushed up the stairs, convinced that the ghosts lying in wait would seize and punish me for my misdeeds.

I fled because ghosts don't believe the kind of lies I habitually told in self-defence. I told more of them than Pinocchio, and without his good reasons. I lied with yes's and no's, because the naked truth seemed ugly to me and because people, unlike ghosts, believe others' lies just as they believe their own. In modern times, I'd have ended up at an analyst's. But my father detected the sign of an artistic vocation in these bad habits.

It's an art, lying, which should be taught in primary schools along with the alphabet, and studied in universities like rhetoric was in antiquity. It's universally prized and should not be left to spontaneity. Whereas in poetry it is said that life is the shadow of a fleeting dream,* in prose we can say it's a concocted lie.

When, one day, my prison guards found me in possession of a map of their headquarters, I put this art to good use, narrating in great detail the story of a treasure

---

* A line from the poem 'Jaufré Rudel' (1888) by Giosuè Carducci.

hunt by students of the neighbouring high school. I didn't convince them, but I planted a seed of doubt, like the child who denies having gone on the sly to see forbidden films— *Frankenstein* and *The Invisible Man*, *Doctor Jekyll* and *Doctor Mabuse*.

Ukzukdum

VII

I looked up to Ukzukdum the black, who was a year older than me and braver in every respect. He was cheerful and sociable but didn't live to roam. In his attic, he had a chemical laboratory and some mechanical equipment that amused him more than anything else.

I envied this vocation of his. I didn't know how to prove Pythagoras' theorem by drawing triangles in the sand; I didn't know how to repair a bicycle tyre with liquid sealant; I preferred a raft to a propeller boat and a peashooter to a rifle. Like Chaplin's tramp, I distrusted the gears of modern times before they even existed.

Of course, Ukzukdum wasn't black and wasn't called that. He was dark-skinned like many of his fellow countrymen and agile like an African boxer who was famous at the time. So I'd given him that nickname as a badge of honour.

His speciality was fireworks, bangers and rockets he set off from the house roof or city ramparts. Sometimes they swerved in unintended directions, but they often flew high with spectacular results. Not like my childish paper arrows.

I spent summer mornings whistling under his windows and we went down to the sea together. One morning I didn't whistle. I was alone when I got off the tram in front of the coloured beach huts. The agitated voice of a girl, our mutual friend, reached me from behind and gave me the news.

But it just wasn't plausible that Ukzukdum was dead. You don't die a week after graduating from the *ginnasio*.* I didn't stop but went into the lido, climbing over the railings as was our wont. I leapt into the water and swam towards the wooden diving board from which my friend used to dive in, making numerous somersaults.

He'd died in his attic grinding his powders in a marble pestle. The concoction was very potent and the pestle burst into a thousand pieces, mutilating his body and opening a gash in the roof. To hide his mutilated arm, they dressed the corpse with the musketeer's gloves worn in student parades.

I remember the funeral, the steps in the new part of the cemetery, the stone with the proud inscription under the name and dates—high-school student. Many years later, I returned to the spot certain of its location but after a long search found nothing. Perhaps a transfer had taken place.

I don't know if I took that swim because I was wicked at heart or to suppress death for a second time. I don't

---

* At the time of Pintor's writing, secondary schooling in the humanities was divided between five years of *liceo ginnasiale* and three further years of *liceo classico*.

think that if I had whistled under the windows I would have changed one destiny. I don't think anything. Perhaps as a grown-up he'd have invented the computer and persuaded me to use it.

VIII

When in 1939 thunder began to roll over the continent, we sought refuge in the interior of the island, like at the time of the Moorish invasions. For me it was my last game in the Garden of Eden in the company of two twins, a country girl and some hapless animals.

I thought I loved animals. I was moved by famous and lesser-known books that talked about them and I protected them from the slingshots of my peers at personal risk. This allowed me to redeem my sins and feel generous. When one day I realized there was no way I could defend the Japanese lizards, I experienced the first internationalist disappointment of my life.

The country girl didn't appreciate these fine feelings. She requested tests of strength from me and the twins, making us lift her with outstretched arms, so that her youthful body adhered to ours; and promised favours to the one who proved most expert at catching lizards. That was how I became a mercenary.

The young temptress was also a skilled rider and, so as not to look bad in her eyes, I practised on the carthorse of a peasant who rented it out after the day's work. It was a jaded beast which, ten metres out of the stable, refused to go any further with an idle child on its back. One day it kicked me with good reason while I was mounting, receiving in exchange from its master so many lashes that its nostrils bled and its hair was matted red.

I felt great shame and withdrew into my French studies, because in the city I had an ill-disposed teacher. For good measure I did the exam in the provinces with an emaciated youth who resembled Giacomo Leopardi. When I got the translation wrong, he smiled at me amiably and gave me a good mark, with the wish that, in contrast to what would soon be his lot, I wouldn't have to go off to war.

The war was distant but you could sense it in the air even in that village. One morning a motorcyclist appeared with a message from my career soldier uncle, who had arrived on the island to inspect coastal defences and was coming to see us. He didn't turn up and the coastal defences did not withstand comparison with the prehistoric nuraghes* and Saracen towers. My uncle left in haste and the commander of the local army corps was pensioned off.

A steamer brought me back with my sisters to the capital we'd left fifteen years earlier. The lifts and phones, the squares and buildings, the fountains and cupolas made the same impression on me as the one experienced by the lord of the apes when he descended from the trees and returned to live on the Greystoke estate.

---

* Megalithic structures, resembling truncated mediaeval towers, erected in Sardinia during the Nuragic Age (1900–730 BCE).

IX

I'd completed high school and reached my eighteenth birthday when my funeral was publicly announced. A hitch disrupted it, like my baptism. Maybe that's why I don't like ceremonies, baptismal or funerary, sacred or profane.

It was 1944, a Roman spring without flights of swallows, when to die young was normal. To miss the opportunity was an unforgivable sin. I'd have left the trepidations and wonders of childhood intact behind me and wouldn't have gropingly embarked on the paths of adult life.

At the last moment, as in a Louisiana prison, chance granted me a reprieve that I calculate equal to two billion heartbeats. As a child, the inconsistency and precariousness of all living things distressed me and now, after this quirk of fate, I would no longer know how to distinguish between fact and fiction. Just because the death doesn't end up in the registry office, it doesn't mean it hasn't occurred.

The city was transfigured then; swarms of black crosses and white skulls had invaded it, flooding the streets and taking the inhabitants' breath away. I remember it well. But our descendants don't like this talk, regarding the past as an invention of their ancestors; and I no longer feel a desire to contradict them. Even the history professors, glasses round their neck, assure me it was all a blunder and that it's no use objecting 'I was there.'

I don't actually deserve the censure of posterity, because in those circumstances I did nothing objectionable. It's true I wanted to throw grenades, but I didn't have any. It's true I set up ambushes, but with a water pistol. These are school memories, like my prisons.

Which don't merit a name from the Risorgimento. It wasn't the Spielberg* that received me, but a boarding house with a garden and a coal hole as spacious as my grandmother's cellar. The toilet under the stairs was damp because the rusty pipes were leaking. But there was sleeping room for two. My schoolmate in one corner, when you looked closely, was losing less blood than in a B-movie. His guard was happy to have killed a Jewish teacher in a building entrance and let his euphoria be known. The uniformed lieutenant, who wielded the horse-whip upstairs, was a patriot in his heart of hearts and would be a senator today.

Where the detached house with garden once was I now find the glass-and-cement headquarters of a joint-stock company. I prefer to remember the city jail where

---

* A reference to the Špilberk Castle in Brno, Southern Moravia, where Austrian authorities imprisoned Italian Carbonari who fought for independence. The poet Silvio Pellico wrote his *Le Mie Prigioni* (1832, *My Prisons*; also translated as *My Ten Years' Imprisonment*) about his time there.

the bugs were just as numerous but innocuous, and where two lifers dressed in stripes provided me with a new pallet. When I left, I thanked them with three banknotes I'd sewn into my jacket in case of emergency. I remember it because it was a case of the kind of reciprocal benevolence that doesn't occur outside a prison or a hospital.

The Postcard

X

A gifted acquaintance of mine didn't pass up the opportunity to die young. One might say he caught it on the wing. At the time it seemed like a terrible trick on his part but I now see things in a different light.

He detested decadence and constraints and I can't image him as an octogenarian in the twilight of the century. Cemeteries where flowers rot weren't to his taste and he found a resting place at the foot of beautiful mountains. That unusual name of his sits well on a gravestone overrun by grass where nothing can be made out any longer.

No one could understand why a happy young man, capable of frequenting the Goddess of Reason and romantic heroines with equal familiarity, went off to meet his end in a minefield. He explained very clearly that he didn't want to remain seated on a stove writing trivia while the world burnt; and that he preferred to do something suited to the circumstances. But no one believes this simple explanation.

I can translate it differently. As a child, he wanted to fly out of windows and believed it possible to conquer sleep by keeping his feet in a bowl of cold water. But he was also very reflective and preferred hugging the walls of the house and circling the rooms to crossing through them. Until he did.

Prior to his adventure he happened to travel with a German paratrooper, a Viking covered in crosses and armbands with three brothers dead in Russia, a veteran of three fronts awaiting his posting to the western front. At the station, they bid each other farewell by drinking a cognac. Such were the circumstances, forgotten today, in which, without too much difference, you could be chatting on a train or shooting at one another in a valley.

I don't think he would appreciate the zeal of friends and family who compiled his posthumous papers. Anyone who wanted to could find them for themselves, scattered as they were. You can't reassemble a person like you do a pithecanthropus, gluing its bones together for the curiosity of visitors.

He had foreseen a violent death for himself; so it was a suicide. He had crossed the front twice; so it was an excess. Those with special qualities should not expose themselves on the front line; so it was a mistake. Thus whisper passing clergymen.

It's impossible to discover a connection between the honest intentions of those years and the dark forest in which the century is ending its course. That's why a timely exit from the stage no longer seems to me a bad trick but a good solution, a good way of avoiding the disillusions of history, leaving all the fun to one's descendants.

The night before, by improvised means, he sent a postcard with the bewigged image of J. S. Bach, which he'd found in the rubble of a farmhouse. It's remained like an heirloom at the bottom of a drawer, next to a letter that our mother sent to a primary school for a commemorative ceremony. The pupils are not to forget, during the eulogy, that the valiant fallen soldier was a young man like them— younger, in fact, the youngest person she'd ever known.

XI

Perhaps I wouldn't have thrown grenades even if I'd had an arsenal full of them. Were I capable of translating an intention into action, I wouldn't be able to say that I've done nothing in my life. I don't know if I should be cheered by this incongruity or ashamed of it.

They made the rounds of the city in five green-and-black taxis, forming a patrol as in cop films. They combed the streets slowly, looking for suspects. They didn't wear uniforms but carried weapons in their belts or on the seats like bank robbers.

I monitored their movements, took notes and drew a map of the area, which was unnecessary and was to cost me dear. I felt safe because I had a document that understated my age, exempting me from conscription, and because the red-haired informer who guided them didn't know me.

I contemplated blocking the motorcade at a cross-roads with a barrow full of household objects and throwing five of those German grenades that looked like bottles. It wasn't an original plan, but I was counting on surprise. Guerrilla warfare and the picture house vied for precedence in this fantasy of mine.

I was disappointed when I came to learn that the underground organization had been broken up, that there weren't any grenades, and that we were to make do with homemade tools, also so as not to involve possible passers-by. But a commando of two boys and one girl against twenty professionals, with unequal arms, was an idea too stupid even for someone like me.

I then thought it better to confront the red-haired man on the Number 16 tram. Someone had seen him get on that tram and it was a question of waiting for a suitable occasion. But hair colour wasn't enough; I would have to address him by name before firing and I don't doubt he would have fired first. I saw myself at the end of the line in a pool of blood amid frightened passengers and fleeing passers-by.

Everything was very concrete, like in dreams. I thought it was vital to accept this challenge; that with these plans I'd change the course of events, encourage the underground organization and facilitate the city's insurrection in advance of the arrival of the rescuing armies. Maybe it was even true.

Sometimes I blame my military uncle. He had influence over the royal family, which sent wreaths with coats of arms and gold ribbons to his funeral. They were quite a sight when I hung them in the bathroom like aristocratic ribbons. If he'd stayed alive, he would have saved me unnecessary trouble. I've no doubt that he would have preserved military honour, that he would have lent an ear to the advice of the conspirators, that the five divisions lined up on the hills of the capital would have moved at his command, that the city would not have fallen and we'd have almost won the war. These things were not to be left in inexperienced hands.

The Toy Soldier

XII

I prefer not to remember his name or physiognomy, except for his bright eyes and a tuft of hair. But I'd recognize his absent-minded step and the woollen overcoat he wore in all weathers, and which he'd wear even today.

His habits were different from ours. High school bored him and he preferred bookstalls. His pockets were full of cigarette stubs to get round rationing and he knew how to get into the cinema without a ticket. He knew the neighbourhood's secrets and for that reason I'd granted him, in his native dialect, the title of monsignor.

When the city grew dark, even he lost his nonchalance. He too thought that the air of the streets had been stolen and he reacted as if it was a personal insult. He couldn't bear this armed intrusion—the swarm of black insignia, the raucous shouting, the orders which would reach you when your back was turned, the daily humiliations.

He'd long harboured the hidden temptation to change the world, but now he banished any hesitation. He ventured out into the open, exposed himself to many dangers, and didn't obey the wise rules of conspiracy because it wasn't in his nature to do so. I had no doubt that, at this rate, things would end badly for him and for me.

Some nights he took refuge in my grandmother's house, with the complicity of the old housekeeper who was fond of him and supplied him with anti-asthma cigarettes. But he kept his bad habit, which we shared, of frequenting the news-stand under his house every morning. He fell into this trap. They imprisoned him and broke his ribs, and didn't kill him out of distraction.

He regained his freedom as though he had an outstanding bill to pay. He didn't calm down until he put on a military uniform that made him look like the good soldier Schweik in the drawings of the time. I am that Schweik—he bid farewell to me bound for the front—who went round the city with his nose in the air and is now off to serve. He was killed by shrapnel in the closing days of the war.

I often ask myself what the effect on him would be, could he see it, of the expanse of dry mud that covers the promised lands. He'd struggle to recognize the young society beyond the ocean that filled us with such enthusiasm at the cinema, with its dancers and pioneers. He wouldn't find in any atlas the legendary city in the east that buried 147,000 Aryan warriors in the snow. He'd seek in vain to understand where the coloured flag hoisted in glory by a soldier on the Scaean Gate ended up. That society has lost its convivial mask; that city has lost its famous name; that flag has been lowered from every mast.

I would like to talk about these things in the shadow of the news-stand, which is still there. Perhaps this metamorphosis, this phantasmagoria, would leave him incredulous; perhaps it'd make him sad; perhaps it'd amuse him. We can't know, because, despite the songs still sung in ceremonies and barracks, graves remain sealed and martyrs don't rise from the dead.

The Circle

XIII

I was sure that war would be the last in the history of the species. An absolute struggle between good and evil does not allow repeat performances. The world was choosing between salvation and damnation and would emerge cleansed by the Flood. It wasn't only me who thought so; everyone did, even if I no longer meet anyone in the streets who remembers this.

If it wasn't the Flood, it looked a lot like it. It raged in the heavens and on earth and everywhere like a deity. It didn't sweep through a continent or an ocean but through the whole globe. It wreaked havoc on men and women of every colour and language. It didn't appear from afar on screens but entered houses through their roofs.

Every generation has its naiveties and falls into some snare or other. But no one, not even the most disabused of men or the devil himself, could imagine that forty million corpses would be dumped like a pile of slag and forgotten the next day.

They called it the Second World War and this should have aroused suspicion. All wars are numbered precisely so as not to fall into error. Numbers are infinite and wars are serial like rosary beads, the pages of a calendar or the twelve-tone scale.

In their imagination, young romantics turned to the Napoleonic battlefields as to the beds of noblewomen; and I can play the same game with at least ten consecutive wars. It isn't an easy exercise, because history reshuffles the meaning of all wars at will. But it's still possible to distinguish them through the variety of forms assumed in each by the practice of death inflicted and endured.

In no field do human beings demonstrate creativity equal to that lavished on European trenches, Ethiopian plains, Spanish villages, Latin American colonies, Asian forests, African deserts or Balkan backyards. Every advance in techniques, and especially in ethics, finds its mirror in wars. A hierarchy of horrors can be adopted, like a seismic scale, to measure the degree of evolution of the species.

But primacy is due to my war, because it encapsulated all the others, past and future. Its genesis and seal, truly worthy of a god, made devastation and annihilation a founding principle of superior civilizations and moulded the future we live in to perfection.

Black-and-white photos in the dust of the archives show men and women slowly emaciated behind barbed wire or incinerated at a stroke in the immolation of their cities. Colour footage on the news shows, above all, children slaughtered in every way, in suburban streets or TV studios, in impoverished lands or in the shadow of skyscrapers, under bombs or among the garbage, in open display or private settings. Past and present form a rounded circle like Giotto's O.

The Devil

XIV

I know nothing about philosophy or science or anything else. I've remained at the first kind of knowledge. I make do with sensory perception; for me, the sun sets in the sea and the moon comes out in the evening and beholds the deserts. So I was taught by a bad teacher who, as a young man, wrote an astronomical treatise but then came to view the nocturnal sky and the Little and Great Bears with different eyes.

So I don't know if war is a military projection of politics, if it depends on modes of production, if it's a phenomenon of intra-species selection. For me, it's inscribed in the heart of man and beats in unison. Peace plays the role of rests in music and is engraved on sarcophagi.

When war doesn't rouse nations, it thrills individuals, spilling over into the details of existence, nesting under the blankets, stalking the streets of the metropolis. It can be sensed without difficulty in the eyes of people rushing about. It then assumes the chivalric name of competition or the vulgar one of domination, and noisily invades the bread or fish market without requiring the shedding of blood but keeping the desire for it warm.

Perhaps it would be beneficial to look at ourselves in this mirror and abandon penitential tears. The rows of white crosses that simulate equality beneath the earth in military cemeteries, and the praises of the Lord that simulate pity on earth between clouds of incense—they don't execrate war, they cultivate it as a faith.

This *perpetuum mobile* convinces me of the anthropological superiority of fascisms of every stripe and time. And it makes me dissent from that gentle thinker who abandoned mathematical certainties to embark on a study of the soul; and concluded that man is neither an angel nor a devil but the two locked in struggle, an incomprehensible being anxious to be reunited with his creator.

This human two-sidedness is nothing more than a theatrical creation that ensures the success of religions, just as the fairy tale of man who is naturally good but historically bad provides work for philosophy. But two-legged man doesn't know these abstractions, is self-contented, regards himself as similar to his creator, considers creation his personal property and aspires to eternity in order to be reunited with himself.

Christian morality flatters this *amour propre*, exhorting us to love others as we love ourselves in an egocentric apotheosis. In days of yore, it was preached by a barefoot man who, as a result, wasn't believed; now it dons purple and travels round in an armoured vehicle.

The Misunderstanding (1946)

XV

In the first year of peace I was the sole surviving young male in the family and sold books by instalments to get by. As a sales rep, I already had a future in the world of publishing.

My university studies had foundered on Tiberius Gracchus' agrarian reform and I readily convinced myself I didn't have an academic vocation. The philosophy professor who deemed me brainless, and advised a legal career, was right.

My programme of musical studies—a five-year plan inspired by Soviet steel production—was behind schedule, like any plan worthy of the name. I should have got a degree in piano and commenced composition, proceeding at a dizzy speed. Unlike Joseph Vissarionovich, I lost my war against time.

It then so happened that an old friend invited me to breakfast, offering me immediate enrolment in the category of professional revolutionaries. After baptism and execution, this was the third twist in my life.

I already had experience as an amateur and no exams were required to become a professional. The pay was spartan but more reliable than instalment sales. I'd be able to start a family, not realizing that the careers of father and revolutionary are incompatible. I can't say if I accepted the offer for these trivial reasons or in order to continue the war by other means and thereby justify my survival.

What I didn't expect was that such a special profession, akin to religious vows or the oath of knights of old, could boil down to employment in a bureaucracy or—as was the case for the literate young man that I was—on a paper. It wasn't a minor misunderstanding and it lasted half a century.

Thus I began to build my house of cards or tarots with all the zeal of an apprentice: investigating the first crime of passion in the post-war period, which involved a blonde woman and a young officer; inquiring into sugar rationing, which was of the first importance; writing press round-ups for eastern bloc embassies, which supplemented my wages; closely monitoring the intentions of the interior minister, to prevent him doing harm in case of emergency; and summarizing the speeches of the top leaders whom I followed on the train, eating sandwiches. They didn't invite me into the restaurant car.

I think I'd have made better use of my time if I'd occupied myself with entomology and with equal diligence studied the society of insects, which has many affinities with ours and has always intrigued me.

The Keyboard

XVI

My music teacher chided me harshly; in his view, I was a victim of moral blackmail. My disguise as a subversive was unnatural and betrayed my true vocation. He was right about the disguise but wrong about the vocation.

I've had five pianos, without knowing how to play any of them. I'm suspected of the opposite in the neighbourhood I live in, because of the low esteem music is held in by educated people. No one who's been through higher education confesses to not knowing about the figurative arts; and any intellectual worthy of the name can pronounce on the restoration of the Sistine Chapel. But they can't distinguish a music score from a hieroglyph.

Vladimir Ilyich cautioned against music because it distracted the mind and softened the heart; and the Chinese drafted resolutions against Franz Schubert, wrongly accusing him of melancholy. This might explain the outcome of the century's great revolutions. But even in common sense there's an incompatibility between politics and music unless it's a question of stirring youthful crowds or accompanying a cavalry charge.

I'd like to confide that there's an insurmountable rivalry between the piano and me. Black and silent, domineering and sardonic, this instrument petrifies me. I was intimidated by even the packing case of my father's piano, abandoned at the bottom of the garden.

I can attempt a psychoanalytic interpretation and blame my first teacher, a viola player in the municipal orchestra, whom I remember with a beard and bow tie. On the third day of lessons he made me turn my back on the keyboard, asking me to distinguish the key by ear. He shook his head and decided I wasn't Amadeus. He was right, but he shouldn't have said it.

The tutor who came up with the musical five-year plan was wiser and, by way of encouragement, made me play on a concert instrument. He told me repeatedly that deafness didn't stop Beethoven, that a small hand can be an advantage if well trained. But nothing could conquer the enmity shown me by those white and black keys. They appear to be eighty-eight but they are many more.

It was a pity because I was full of good will. I took lessons at night and the occupant of the floor above pounded on her saucepans out of spite. In the summer holidays I applied myself by practising on pianos abandoned in sacristies.

But had I disguised myself as a musician, instead of a subversive or entomologist, everyone would've been wise to it from the start of the performance. The Piano and I might be the title of a Buster Keaton film.

The Temple

XVII

1956 was memorable for four reasons: it snowed in Rome in March; there was an unanticipated movement of tanks on the continent; half the world caved in; and the abdomen of my second child became intractable. Among these events, the last was the most important.

The surgeon opened and sewed him up again. It was a mild infection of the mesentery, something I'd never heard of. But pleurisy set in and the emeritus professor at the bedside diagnosed tuberculosis of the membranes and potential meningitis, alluding to my baptism. He was excited by all these conjunctions and gave a lecture at the university on this clinical case.

I engaged in a pitched battle against the mechanicism of the argument and won, since two or even three parallel pathologies need not be connected. From that moment I converted to methodical doubt, forever ceasing to believe that two and two make four; that the wheel of history spins forwards; that progress is measured by stock exchange prices; that the last will be first.

A friend kept me up to date on the deconsecration that was meanwhile shaking the world, in one of those convulsions that agitate history every so often, casting idols down from the altar into the dust. This time it was a gigantic idol, made of steel and marble, who had issued messages of liberation and victory to great multitudes and was now being felled. I understood nothing but was certain that the temple would collapse to the last stone on anyone who profaned it without good reason and without even Samson's understanding.

I was sorry, because in years of iron and fire it was from that temple that salvation from a mortal danger had come; and I too was a grateful idolater. But, above all, it amazed me that half the world had collapsed and its inhabitants continued to walk streets that no longer existed. They mistook an earthquake for a makeover, a confusion no one should indulge in.

They were called communists and had eighty-two delegations in five continents. I once saw them all meeting together minus one, an impressive spectacle. Their death agony would last three decades but the meningitis contracted that year was to carry them all off to the grave or insanity.

From this experience I deduced that political action and intellectual speculation are parasitic in the same way. The latter requires strict habits and well-equipped minds; the former can be performed by sheer intuition and in shirtsleeves. But both ride on the coat-tails of events. They are perched on a branch from which they spy passing earthworms to seize and swallow. Then they return to the branch and start all over again.

Fair Hair

XVIII

The child who recovered from mesentery died forty-one years later. In a diary he called desiderata, because it was full of unrealized plans, I found a record of that first hospital admission. It begins with a quotation from a forgotten poet, 'better to die with fair hair',* and continues as follows:

> A sharp, icy wind brushed my skin, bringing a blush to my cheeks, under my pyjamas and the blanket I was wrapped in. And my father holding me close wasn't enough to warm my body, still less my heart.
>
> I had turned six not long before; it was a particularly cold March (by Roman standards). In a diagnosis that the emergency required to be rapid, or rather rushed, I was found to have peritonitis that only the absence of a high fever and a racing pulse . . . I don't remember the

---

* Giovanni Pascoli, 'L'Aquilone' (1904).

preparations clearly: a phone call to a clinic, a bag for the necessary hospital things packed in haste, being wrapped in a blanket, leaving the house with my father and the doctor, their drawn faces, which I can still see. And over everything, like the soundtrack of a horror film, my tear-choked cry: 'Mom! Mom!' But she didn't come, didn't come that instant, and what persists as an indelible memory is the feeling of the first abandonment (or, perhaps I experienced it thus, the first betrayal) by a person (my mother, that is) on whom I'd heedlessly and utterly relied, almost as if, though long since weaned, I still needed contact with her protective breast.

Clarae et obscurae . . . (to quote Baumgarten[*]) are my memories of that event and the others surrounding it—as though I lived in an 'aesthetic' world, or at least that's how I remember it today. A world of sensations: colours, smells, touches, noises, tastes that only now, decades later, I can rationalize, but without succeeding, even today, in extracting their full meaning.

(Despite, or maybe thanks to, my parents' communist 'faith', my family was patriarchal not just in its forms. But I'll return to this when this patriarchy will assume the shape of a clearly defined, structured grip.) I opened this parenthesis to say that for the first time, very small and

---

[*] Alexander Gottlieb Baumgarten (1714–62) wrote of clear and obscure representations in his *Metaphysics* (1739).

without any preparation, I was carted off from the things I loved, because in them I discovered affections and essences. And it was a trauma that, in a moment whose drama I could read on the faces of my father and mother, I was ripped from the affection of the one so that the other—for him it was almost a duty—could obstetrically pull me out of the uterine walls of my Monteverde home—pulled out by a 'stranger' (I'm not making judgements but reporting feelings) who acted with the same firm and frigid function as forceps. More, a caesarean section that extracted me with violence from the warm amniotic fluid of my bed and mother and flung me into an icy, efficient world of which I remember, above all, the smell of the anaesthetic ether.

For the rest, I can only remember a few small episodes from this hospital admission, almost all of them unpleasant—including, when I was getting a bit better and could get up, seeing Rome turned white by the thick falling snow. An unpleasant episode because in my imagination the snow was a plaything forbidden me at the time. I also remember a considerable quantity of biscuits, which came from the nearby Ruschena cake shop and whose taste I still retain in my mouth.

I wasn't aware that my paternal anxiety didn't convey intimacy and tenderness but estrangement and imposition. And I'd continue to be unaware of it in graver circumstances. Thus it can happen that one brings a child into the world in distress, that one doesn't help him to live in that world, that one makes him grow up in pain and die in solitude.

Kakadu

XIX

We were a very young family—a father and mother, a girl and boy—whose combined age was less than fifty. Too young—like romantic marriages, conjugal precocity should be prohibited.

My old uncle had given me permission to marry, although paternally advising me against it. He said my desire was an emotional rebound from the war, as if I wanted to reanimate the world. On the contrary, I wanted to return to pre-war times out of nostalgia, in search of a lost serenity.

So my children's infancy should have resembled mine, as should their thoughts; the house should have resembled their grandparents'; and the mother should have accustomed herself to memories and milieus that didn't belong to her, but which I thought would compensate her for the poverty she'd grown up in.

Nagging worries guided my pedagogy. I feared accidents, I wielded thermometers, I placed protective nets on the fifth-floor windows, as my father had done round the old garden. I lamented the fact that our second child was unstable on his bike and that the first curled her hair. Inverting a famous saying, I assigned paramount importance to the baggage and thought the rest would take care of itself.

I earned on the sly, because it seemed to me a residue of bourgeois habits. And when, under a false name, I wrote columns in women's papers or telephoned-in reports from Hungary, I felt guilty. I believed I was being considerate but didn't realize that, to a child's eyes, I seemed like 'an older person who was always shouting and was never there'.

The red fish went whirling round in vain. I don't know how otherwise to explain why I didn't teach my offspring the little music I knew, except through the song of the tailor Kakadu, who worked in hell ('Oh tailor what are you doing,/What are you chattering about?/You've got to clothe the devils./What will be will be).* Nor can I say why our holidays weren't on the happy isle but in a built-up resort on the Adriatic railway line that I reached in a Lambretta crossing the peninsula. I used to drive under the August sun with a paper hat on my head.

When adversity shattered this little domestic fish tank, I blamed bad luck. But now I know I don't have any extenuating circumstances and that the fourth commandment wasn't written for me.

---

* From the 'Kakadu Variations', Beethoven's op. 121, a piano trio (1824), which sets to music a theme from an opera by Wenzel Müller.

Pasture

XX

Ten years after the collapse of the temple, one April morning in 1966, I threw open the windows and realized I was living in a house surrounded by pear trees. The perfume of the bushes informed me I'd returned to the island of the Moors.

If the scrivener listening to me should ask the reason for this fairy-tale move, I'd be in a spot. Of the previous ten years I recall nothing, for the excellent reason that I did nothing except build my house of cards ten storeys high and acquire fame as a scourge of modern mores. Until an edict obliged me to replace the urban glass harmonica with a country panpipe.

These were edicts that emanated from remote places, Tibetan fora and conventicles so important that no one remembers them. I was an adult and don't know why I submitted to such treatment. Luckily, I found the sheep very friendly.

Perhaps I was imitating Cincinnatus. The neighbouring village offered no more than a bar with a pinball machine and a store that sold tomatoes. Beyond the provincial road was the sea and a seaweed beach with some houses under construction. The salt rusted abandoned machinery and rotted my bedsheets.

The peasant house was inhabited by its owners, who set aside three rooms for me. One entered it down a drive and through a farmyard populated by hens and cats, like the ravine at the bottom of my childhood garden. I was well supplied with eggs and salted throstles, but there too I wrote anonymous articles to make ends meet.

I knew of Carlo Felice because of the monument in the city where the taxis parked. I now studied his agrarian reform (following that of Tiberius Gracchus), which imposed land enclosures on the island to discourage sheep-farming and promote cultivation. I precisely calculated the annual yield of a sheep with variations in the rental of pasture; I sided with the shepherds against the tenants; and I imagined the island flourishing with grasslands and thriving herds.

I considered invading the regional government buildings with the flocks to have them graze on their tapestries and I visited the breeders of Polish sheep to educate myself. I was dumbfounded when an emigrating shepherd told me he preferred the silicosis of Belgian mines to the transhumance he recalled from his island childhood.

I frequented the house of an Armenian doctor who was attempting to civilize the mental patients' ward in the city hospital, and who was thus an appropriate interlocutor in the circumstances. I confided in him, as I'm now doing with the scrivener, to avert the melancholy that descended upon me in the evenings.

The melancholy came when I slowly walked back up the alleys I'd gone down with youthful self-confidence and when I found the ramparts—on which I'd lorded as a child—to be damaged and deserted. I didn't recognize myself in these twilight strolls; the connections evaded me and I asked myself where the swallows' cries had gone and why no one played with ninety-cent rubber balls.

The Clock

XXI

Perhaps I should have stayed round those parts and learnt to do something else. For example, fishing like someone I know who now works amid corals and lobsters rather than at a lathe. But I didn't have that education and returned to the big city where I wasn't wanted.

I continued to indulge the most contrived of pretences, that things were different from how they are. I continued not to understand that if dogs have bent legs, crabs walk sideways and moles are short-sighted, they're fine that way.

The year 1969 had arrived and the snow once again fell in abundance. In a turreted city, another of those Tibetan conventicles was underway, where I was to announce two revolutionary discoveries: that there weren't any living communisms on earth, just as there's no water on the moon; and that the historical conjunction of a Capricorn and a Virgo would have engendered monsters. These were discoveries that exposed one to exile, like Galilean physics in its time.

I had to present myself for the examination early in the morning and spent the night reflecting in a hotel where a large clock struck the hours with the sound of a bell. I had a spare stopwatch to time the speech I was due to give—19 minutes and 25 seconds speaking slowly, with 35 seconds leeway vis-à-vis the rules of the confraternity.

In the huge hall there was a mortuary chill. There was silence in the stalls and murmuring in the galleries. Present on the decked-out platform was the solemn of leaderships. Lined up on the right were Siberian delegations attuned to the ice of the hall and the snow of the city.

On this occasion I discovered the great importance of bells. I don't mean electric bells but the bronze ones that are rung by shaking them. It's an object that withstands time, like the stamp of post-office clerks or the hammer of judges. It's used universally, in courts and churches, schools and parliaments.

It's well-known that any speech is particularly dependent on its conclusion. My closing words were soaring, appealing to collective intelligence and communal spirit, when the chairman's ringing brought them to the ground like a burst of machine-gun fire.

My stopwatch indicated 19 minutes and 10 seconds; technically, I was right, but I was wrong in principle. Some Indian delegates whispered in the gallery and, head bowed, I went out into the snow.

XXII

I don't recall any childhood trauma connected with printed paper. News-stands and tobacconists' windows with illustrated newspapers attracted me but I preferred the picture house. So it wasn't out of a maniacal impulse that, having spent nineteen years on one newspaper, I decided to spend twenty-five on another.

Perhaps it was a form of revenge on my old employers and their confraternity, which committed mass suicide twenty years later. Perhaps I sought a refuge or a purpose, perhaps I believed in freedom in one printing house. Perhaps I offered those who wanted it a less bloody weapon than those that would soon be in fashion. Perhaps I was enjoying a second youth and venturing out on the open sea.

It was the year 1971 and our paper boat was buffeted by blustering winds. There weren't any rich ship-owners or indigenous patrons, Spanish sovereigns or Chinese emperors, willing to subsidize a navigation plotted on a nautical map dating from 1848. But I counted on favourable seas to drive us towards new horizons.

As ever, I was wrong. The tides ebbed and the horizon literally turned leaden.* The boat would never put out to sea. It hugged the coast for thousands of miles, never anchoring in welcoming ports, and would end up losing its bearings.

My fault—I thought I knew how to stay at the helm by dint of extensive training, but I was mistaken even in this. Everyone on board knew more about it than me— boatswains and cabin boys, engineers and cooks, old sea dogs or greenhorns; and each of them pursued their preferred course.

I thought I was the teacher, at least when it came to stringing words together and handling tarot cards. But not even this was true. Playing in the hold with the crew on nine thousand consecutive evenings, I lost the whole stock of eloquence accumulated over the years, like the inept Spanish captain of the San Dominick who ended up his own prisoner.**

According to Admiral Lord Nelson, 'any sailor who attacked a fort was a fool'. It's a verdict I found transcribed on a map of the Cyrenaican coastline at the back of a family bookshelf. I'll cap it by asserting that any sailor who sails in shallow waters is a drunk.

---

* A reference to the *anni di piombo*, or years of lead, the period of terrorism, counter-terrorism and state terrorism that more or less overlaps with the Italian seventies.

** An allusion to Herman Melville's novella *Benito Cereno* (1856).

I don't know for certain if the boat I'm talking about is still seaworthy or will end up being decommissioned. I'd be sorry because its hull has come through many trials. When it was launched by disreputable shipyards, no one believed it capable of staying afloat for more than six months. It was a miracle of naval engineering and perhaps the only error was not to fly the white flag, which is always welcome in sea ports.

The Park

XXIII

There's a park in a border town I used to visit regularly (not any more—I prefer an Augustan Protestant cemetery that's not far away). It's an unkempt park with a few benches and some uninhabited structures. There I met people who talked to themselves, like we all do in secret, and a wise old ghost whom I knew when he was alive.

An habitual visitor, a postman in the city, goes to the park early in the morning to meet an emperor from whom he expects honours and riches. He says that, in their heart of hearts, all normal people anticipate honours and wealth from an emperor; or thanks to luck, because toil doesn't deliver these goods. The difference with normal people is that he isn't in a hurry and, while waiting, is content with a cigarette.

On other occasions I met a woman of indeterminate age, toothless as happens to the poor, who always carried with her a naked celluloid doll, heedless of bad weather. In her company I understood I'd never been poor and never succeeded in becoming such.

If I hadn't been just passing by but there because of personal misfortune, someone would immediately have come to my aid to restore normality. By contrast, no one came to her aid. Thus I know I've continually reflected on the world's sorrows and miseries without having any experience of them and hence any knowledge.

The ghost I knew when he was alive comes from very far off to aid me, as he's always done in difficult times. He's an old gentleman with a long overcoat and felt hat, which he raises in an unfashionable gesture of greeting. He approaches in small steps, his shoulders bent by an immaterial burden, and carries a book of mediaeval lyrics under his arm. Some call him Romeo da Villanova (Dante's *Paradiso*, VI), but I know he had a different, unlucky name.

The leading philosophers of the time turned to him for advice; and his hospitable house, where the spirits of his ancestors hovered, was the destination of masters and pupils of opposing schools whom the old sage coaxed into tolerance. But it was also the destination of a variegated humanity—emigrant peasants, fallen soldiers, impoverished widows.

Over long years of study, he collected and arranged 300,000 entries for an encyclopaedic work that met with censorship and never appeared. On his deathbed he went in search of these tampered pages, and, in his delirium, demanded their restitution. At his bedside he didn't have speeches by masters and pupils but a maid noticed that his hands, crossed on his chest, were as white as snow because they knew no evil.

When the coffin left the house, twelve soldiers who'd turned up from the nearby barracks presented arms. No one knows who'd summoned them and no one knows the reason for that salute. On returning from the funeral, his old sister changed the water in a vase of tuberoses, tidied the kitchen, stretched out gracefully on her bed and died.

XXIV

When, from the vantage-point of age, I watch the world (or its parody) go round on small screens, it looks to me like a huge slaughterhouse set on a giant rubbish dump. I see it finally bound in fraternity under these two ensigns. But this is an unpleasant point of view and so I don't insist.

Since that's how things are, I no longer have cause to fear a witch carrying me off to another world; I don't pause to count my heartbeats; I don't get agitated at the idea of a planetary explosion, which seems plausible to me. An expert on bipeds like Dr Lorenz* actually places that eventuality last among the eight cardinal sins of humanity and perhaps he's right. The explosion has already occurred and repeat performances are futile.

I have a suggestive passport that expires in 2001. I await that date in a relaxed frame of mind because, as Seneca writes to Lucilius, death isn't in front of me but behind me, in the time used up. The child who still plays in these pages

---

* Konrad Lorenz (1903–89), Austrian ethologist.

died long ago. So even the grave frightens me less and I shan't leave minute instructions for a pyre on the Ganges or a pit in Spoon River.

When on sunny Sundays my father took me with him to visit the tomb of his three brothers, who died before he was born, there were three marble cherubs whom I identified with the little brothers, laid in the earth but likewise desirous of putting on wings and flying away. Today, I don't have such raw sensations. And I think that even the earth can be soft.

But I'm not indifferent to the ways in which people pass on. It shouldn't be slow and painful, as I've witnessed. Nor should it be domestic, because that's anachronistic, or take place in a hospital, because that's desolate. It should be brisk, like anything modern, and suited to each individual.

One afternoon, sixty years ago, a Piedmontese girl who now has a bar in the village square heard a rumble of thunder and looked up at the sky. She saw a military aeroplane emerging from the clouds trailing smoke and circling in search of somewhere to crash-land. An explosion blew off a wing that started to gyrate, with a man clinging on to belts and ropes. The aircraft plunged into a swamp.

An act of sabotage, thought the girl; and she still does. A very fitting death for the severe general who intimidated me, with his silver stripes and clinking sabre, even when he took me to ice-cream parlours. I can see him issuing calm orders to the military crew in a concerted effort to extinguish the fire and land. One of his forearms remained attached to the plane's controls.

The Exhortation (2001)

XXV

Now that the scrivener has finished recording these confidences, and I reread them as set down haphazardly in chapters, I realize I can't go on in this way. It turns out that not only have I done nothing in my life but I'm ending it in a dark mood. It's not okay—Miss Marianne Kirchgessner* played a feeble instrument but didn't sound a wrong note. That's why Mozart and Beethoven wrote for her.

I'd like to take my leave by dispelling this impression. Dark moods are widespread and, in highly developed countries, ensure the success of analysts and pharmacists. I don't deny one has often accompanied my walks, but I left it on a park bench and am now courting comedy.

Intentions count more than ever. If it was for the sake of the results, I wouldn't redo anything I have and haven't done. I'd prefer not to. But when it comes to intentions it's

---

* Pintor misremembers her name as Sofia.

another story. The rumour that the road to hell is paved with good intentions is spiteful. Outcomes are disappointing and ephemeral. Good purposes instead are like a pollen that never blossoms but scents the air.

I'd advise a sentimental revolution. Of all the revolutions or reformations, plebeian or aristocratic, proletarian or bourgeois, cultural or moral, none has ever been conceived as sentimental. Perhaps because the emotions, understood as relations between people, are difficult to clone and reputed to be feminine in gender.

I'd advise a retractile revolution—though the adjective doesn't lend itself to mural inscriptions—one that restores inner rhythms and inner restraints, abolishing clocks. Something that makes it possible to understand one another with smoke signals, the guttural calls of gorillas, caresses and blows, the gestures that brush living things and inanimate ones, and say more than the articulate words we are so proud of.

It may be one of those anecdotes to which the ignorant reduce history but I seem to remember that a celebrated revolutionary regarded it as a crime to crush an insect needlessly. Perhaps this mentality led to her ending up in pieces in a canal, but it seems like a good example with which I say my goodbyes.

Not without recalling the exhortation by Anonymous quoted at the start, which I remain attached to after all. The author adds that, if one is pessimistic about man, one might as well tie a stone round one's neck and throw oneself into the sea. So it is. His exhortation resembles the wish for a rapid recovery addressed to an incurably ill person. But there are wishes it's right to make, even if they don't achieve the desired end.

The Medlar Tree

Narrow is the leaf, broad is the way . . .*

---

* *Stretta è la foglia / larga è la via*—a traditional Tuscan ending for
fairy tales.

1997

June

Giano is one hundred years old and has decided to sit under a medlar tree to count the days, no longer succumbing to worldly temptations. It seems to him a sensible decision, appropriate to the circumstances. He will do nothing and let his thoughts wander beyond the foliage, like clouds.

Summer is a season that fosters this state of mind. The chestnut and beech trees of the hills offer more shade than a medlar, but Giano's preference for this wretched tree derives from the fact that he used to have one in the garden of his house. Among its branches blossom memories that are more agreeable than anything else.

It's strange that the old man has survived despite being a hardened smoker. As a child, he bought pestiferous cigarettes from soldiers who received them as rations and sold them cheaply. Otherwise he recycled his father's dog-ends, cleaning out the ashtrays. In hard times, he used ground dry leaves and poppy seeds.

At the registry office it turns out that Giano isn't so far in his years. Even his acquaintances are dubious; he seems addled but in good health. But the word of a gentleman counts for more than a birth certificate and is to be respected.

Much of his life has found him shut up in a room, writing in newspapers against something or someone. By temperament and profession he was a polemicist (a natural contrarian, as one might say of an unruly child). What he did was of no use, but it seemed to him of great significance and he was utterly devoted to his revolutionary vocation. To write aimlessly or daydream under a tree does indeed have a use—smoking fewer cigarettes.

A famous novelist used a cigarette holder forty centimetres long to avoid getting smoke in his eyes. But Giano smokes unusually thin tapered cigarettes and you can't buy a cigarette holder of that diameter. You'd have to search for it in a Chinese bazaar.

The old man has never been to China and doesn't intend to go there for such a trifle. Unlike in the past, today it wouldn't be a journey to the mysterious Orient. Countries have become bazaars which all resemble one another. It wouldn't be like venturing forth to discover the sources of the Nile or the ruins of Troy. The few journeys Giano has undertaken in his life have almost invariably been disappointing, lacking the surprises he anticipated, as if he already knew the places he visited and the people he met. He once happened to eat a ram's eye at the table of Asiatic shepherds, but that's the only adventure he can recount.

This loss of marvel, of surprise, of the unexpected revelation of unknown things, is the fault or merit of the cinema. Already as a child, in the dark of a provincial cinema, he'd toured the world in his imagination, from tropical forests to African deserts, from polar icecaps to metropolitan skyscrapers, all for the price of 75 cents. It was like seeing the future in a magic lantern.

One can forgive the twentieth century everything, even the two world wars and the ones that followed, even fashion shows and Formula One races, but not the sin of having sacrificed cinema to television. The latter is an empty box that displays a world as flat as a blackboard and doesn't distinguish between a scene of war and a game of soccer. There's the same difference between the two screens as between the heat of a fireplace and a disconnected fridge.

To tell the whole truth, spaghetti with salmon and the last movement of the Ninth Symphony used as an advertising jingle are also unforgivable.

July

Giano is expecting bad news and can't get this expectation out of his head even under the shade of the medlar. It's not a happy state of affairs. Listening to music would be a good remedy, but in the open air sounds scatter and in the city there's such a din that even music becomes just one more noise. Sounds demand a silence and a space that can't be found anywhere and which can't be carved out by putting a bug in one's ear.*

G. K. Chesterton, a man of wit, felt a surge of respect for the human race only when opening a railway timetable. A classical orchestra is as intricate as a railway timetable but certainly more beautiful and deserving more than respect.

The eye aids the ear, and you have to observe in an empathetic spirit the players and their magical instruments performing the miracle. High on the right, over the proscenium of a village hall, a very graceful girl plays the bassoon and one wonders about the reason for her choice.

---

* An acerbic reference to headphones that also plays on the expression *mettere la pulce nell'orecchio a qualcuno*, meaning to arouse someone's suspicions.

Perhaps it was played by her father, or her mother (unlikely), or even her grandfather—a family tradition. It's an instrument that lends itself to chamber music but also to the kind of band concerts you might hear in town squares in summer.

Or else she started out with the flute or clarinet, the solo instruments preferred by composers, falling back on the bassoon out of modesty or because it's easier to find an engagement. Or maybe she's a versatile girl who plays all the wind instruments and alternates them depending on the occasion. It might also simply be that she loves the sound of that wooden cylinder. It has an antique flavour. In a famous fairy tale, it plays the part of the grandfather.*

You don't need to be a fetishist to grant personality and charm to musical instruments. A professional cellist who gave private recitals to supplement his income argued from direct experience that the cello has an irresistibly seductive effect when played in private. Its shape is very beautiful; its sound is full and penetrating; its range is limited but so harmonious as to be self-sufficient.

With these thoughts three cigarettes have gone up in smoke, rather than six. Which means they aren't profound thoughts. But what is a profound thought? Thought can be complex, like chess, but it can't be profound because it thinks itself in a circle and remains on the surface, like an image in a mirror.

---

* A reference to *Peter and the Wolf*, put to music by Prokofiev.

Emotions which seem transient but remain imprinted forever are profound. And however concealed or repressed, they resurface at times, as if by a spell. The occasionally tangled thought of the hunchback of Recanati (or even the hunchback of Ghilarza)* suddenly becomes clear when it's directly related to the turmoil of his soul. And it acquires an appeal speculative philosophies rarely possess.

---

* Giacomo Leopardi and Antonio Gramsci, respectively.

August

Bad news used to arrive by telegram, yellow envelopes delivered in person by the postman which the addressee opened with apprehension. Now they usually come by telephone. So Giano fears the ringing of this device more than any other menace.

One day, on the public phone at a village restaurant, he learnt that someone dear to him was nearing his end in a Roman hospital. His sister had found him slumped over his desk, a farewell note nearby. Exceptionally, the news was broadcast by radio, so that the intensive care doctors applied themselves more than usual and on the third day he came out of the coma. The cock has crowed, announced the nurse. If that lad had been a nobody, he would have died in a corner of the reception ward.

Another summer morning, the phone rang when Giano was leaving the house with two suitcases to go to the seaside. Rather than taking the stairs, he succumbed to the temptation to pick up the receiver and found out that an old friend was dying in a distant hospital. So he set off—not for a holiday but for a funeral.

He also fears phone calls that don't come. One December afternoon the telephone didn't ring. The person who should have called to reassure the family at the end of a journey missed the appointment because his plane had crashed with all its crew.

But that was a different era. Subsequent messages will be precisely recorded on the tape of an answering machine.

There's a protagonist in a short story who wanders country paths in the early morning, filling his lungs with air. He's in good humour, wears a tracksuit and walks briskly to compensate for the ailments of a sedentary existence. The ringing of a telephone, which issues incessantly from a factory window, eventually reaches his ear. The call can't be for him—definitely not—but the ringing is nagging. He gives in, turns back on his steps, climbs through the window and anxiously lifts the receiver to find out what's happened.

Giano doesn't know when the bad news will come. But he knows it will come from a city burdened with too many memories. Today, on the windy seafront of that city, a drowned man was dragged ashore and left on the pavement under a sheet. His presence didn't embarrass the swimmers and it intrigued the children. The morning passed quietly until the arrival of the ambulance, which intrigued the children even more.

The sea at Sapri is clearer than in Trieste, but the shoreline is overhung by a promontory where a train passes every hour. If the holidaymaker is in a good mood, the train amuses him as it enters and exits a tunnel whistling like a toy. If he's in a bad mood, he can't stand the racket and curses the railway system and the disturbed peace. But it's always the same train that passes and it's always the same holidaymaker. This is the theory of relativity applied to the nervous system.

Even here there are glorious reminiscences and one wonders why a valiant man like Pisacane chose Sapri for his enterprise.* He was a student of military affairs and will have had his reasons. But anyone who's been to high school immediately associates that exploit with the 'gleaner' of the homonymous poem** and thinks that 'three hundred young and strong' died because of her. Who knows why that peasant girl is carved in the guise of a siren on a rock in the middle of the sea.

A century later, a gentleman was apprehended in a Roman hotel because he had a reprint on his desk of the essay on revolution written a century earlier by the Neapolitan hero. The police hadn't studied the Risorgimento and regarded it (not without some justification) as a subversive contemporary publication.

Some medals only possess a reverse side.

---

* Carlo Pisacane was a Neapolitan revolutionary in the Italian Risorgimento. The Sapri expedition was a failed attempt to spark an insurrection against the Bourbons in 1857.

** Luigi Mercantini, *La Spigolatrice di Sapri* (1857).

September

'Lord: it is time. The summer was immense./Lay your shadow on the sundials/and let loose the wind in the fields.'*

A poet heralds autumn better than any weatherman.

Fountain pens work badly even with a golden nib. Biros are impersonal and good for filling in a form. The typewriter is professional but doesn't aid reflection and is boring. The computer makes one nostalgic for cave paintings. All excellent reasons not to write.

Some genius should invent the quill pen and the glass inkwell, because they make one meditate and because throwing an inkwell against the wall is a pleasure that should be experienced at least once.

Philologists should verify with what implements Dante Alighieri wrote, and whether he polished his verses only in daylight or by candlelight too. The *Divine Comedy* is too long and few scholars have read the whole of it. To copy it

---

* Rainer Maria Rilke, 'Autumn Day'.

by hand would require years, which pass more quickly today than they did in the Middle Ages. Progress contracts time and shortens life, only appearing to prolong it. How the poet could achieve his work is an enigma of the past.

To write a book in the third millennium requires vast self-regard. It's enough to go into a municipal library and look at a stationer's shop window to realize that the world doesn't need another volume.

For writing in newspapers, by contrast, obtuse stubbornness suffices. If a professional journalist on average writes three typed pages twice a week for fifty years (low average), he will produce fifteen thousand printed pages, equivalent to thirty volumes of five hundred pages each—an encyclopaedia that requires a cabinet all to itself, a monumental work of paper pulp.

In the house of a bibliophile, a bookcase stood out with a complete edition of Giuseppe Mazzini's works. If the austere republican had made do with repeating 'God and the People', he'd be remembered solely for those four words.

Synthesis is poetry and vice versa. The first four verses of the canto dedicated by the hunchback of Recanati to Silvia describe that adolescent in such a way that any sixteen-year-old makes their own mental portrait and would like to meet her in real life in the village streets. Her happy, fugitive eyes are dark like her hair, which is pinned at the neck. She's shy and doesn't want her song, hushed between domestic walls, to be heard by furtive ears.

But in prose too synthesis is commendable. Giano often cites the four apostles, rough and terse, who narrate rather than speculate and prefer parables to concepts. Though banal, it's worth recalling that the Nazarene's good fortune was to have stumbled upon the four best chroniclers in history.

Of Chopin's twenty-four preludes, the seventh is a slow mazurka of seventeen bars. It lasts forty seconds and is probably the shortest piece in the whole of classical music. Even a beginner can play it easily but every concert pianist interprets it differently.

The old man is conscious that to live off memories, as they call it, is to die softly. But that's how it goes, there's no choice. It might look like a voluntary renunciation but it's a law of nature.

Energy, stimuli, goals all fade away. Curiosity fades away, because you've already rummaged everywhere and know things and people, flavours and perfumes, trees and animals, the sea and the moon, dawns and dusks, sleeping and waking, baptisms and funerals, loves and weapons, temples and brothels, right and wrong, Olympics and wars, enthusiasm and disappointment, the ebbs and flows of history.

What relish is there to be had in remembering the white cars of the tram to the seaside? None—if anything, you feel pity, regret, resentment, because you were there then and now you're not. But you would like to return to the scene of the crime and so you meticulously call to mind every detail—the platforms with the handrail, the little gates with their latches, the last stop where the tracks sink into the sand.

Much has been written about senility by Latin philosophers and modern novelists, but it's a condition that can't be understood by proxy. You enter into a body alien and unforeseen. No one can grasp this mutation without experiencing it, just as no one can conceive himself to be an ant without being one.

Pacing about in a smoky room with dark glasses on your nose, cotton in your ears, sand in your mouth, size 48 footwear and a barrel on your back. It's easy to caricature the impediments of age, which are more comical than pathetic.

Humiliation is born from the comparison between before and after. When as a child he rode a bike up forbidding climbs and down steep slopes, or raced his friends come rain or come shine, he was convinced his legs would never let him down and that till the end of time he'd continue to bounce like a ball along the smooth rocks of the Arbatax shore. Now a flight of stairs is enough to arouse his suspicion and he'd never jump like a kangaroo onto the running board of a moving tram.

On his doorstep, with his hands folded on the handle of a walking stick, his head bowed and his body shrunken, a blind old man spends his day on a straw chair. When he hears a footfall, he repeats the same question in a childish voice: If Christ lets so many young people die, why keep me languishing here? One might answer him with a handshake, mumbling words on the human condition and the ways of the Lord, and concluding that God and Satan are twins.

November

Junior died last night, Saturday, 9 November. He died in his sleep, in that distant city he didn't like, at forty-eight years of age. The news arrived by telephone, with two brief recorded messages that didn't go into details.

It was a silent and solitary death, a wary death. They noticed because in the morning the coffee machine wasn't waiting on the kitchen hob as usual. The day before, he'd called to plan a visit to Rome before Christmas. He had a foreboding about death but didn't await it passively. On his desk he left a diary open at the last page:

I must organize (plan) the little time remaining to me in Teutonic fashion. Not in the long term, but day by day. Today, I could spend the morning sketching out the musical article on the deafness of new generations (but that's not exactly the title). I could then resume the autobiography or frame the course on the history of rock for the children in care at Sert* (but I haven't got the

_____

* *Servizi Pubblici per le Tossicodipendenze*, state-funded drug rehabilitation centres.

books). Or finally, I could play, even if I don't know with what methodology. Thus the day will be full . . . of many vacuums—I can't in fact delegate to objects (pens, pianos and what have you) what I've been expecting from people for too long.

It was death by consumption, without a definite cause. The body has been consigned to a morgue; there was no wake; the burial awaits the go-ahead. The room reserved by the main hospital for the ordinary dead is in an empty courtyard; it looks like a garage where the coffins are parked for a few hours, in rapid turnover. Junior was often a patient in that hospital and even now he seems asleep. His eyes shut tight, his thin face, his tall figure—there's no difference. The father thinks of taking him back home with him, as if death had not intervened.

Dealing with practical matters, renting the grave in the Protestant cemetery, collecting the obituaries, tidying up the house in Rome, imagining a possible return once these things have been done. Giano has always acted in this way, convinced that the solution to material problems resolves all the rest. To change would be a betrayal, an abandonment of tried-and-tested habits, a cancellation. Better to repeat the same gestures, to regard this vacuum as a transition and go on speaking at a distance of music and Job.

For Christmas 1985, Giano received an elegant edition of the Bible, with this dedication from Junior: 'For not the hearers of the law are just before God, but the doers of the law shall be justified. For when the Gentiles, which have not the law, do by nature the things contained in the law, these, having not the law, are a law unto themselves: Which shew the work of the law written in their hearts ... [All will become clear in] the day when God shall judge the secrets of men by Jesus Christ according to my gospel' (Romans 2:13–16).

Junior's papers and writings are collected in four boxes. A humorous epitaph on the back of a photograph begins with 'excellent cook' and ends with 'terrible specimen'. At the funeral were children in care with social services with whom he recorded conversations for a book that will not appear. A middle-aged stranger carried under his arm a copy of the music journal Junior published in his youth.

Music as a youthful bond, theology as a search for meaning, integration into the damaged world. In this itinerary there's a logic that makes him say for a moment he's lived 'well and intensely' but made many mistakes and been harshly punished for it.

What's the connection between the blond child who left in a hurry with his sister from the sheds of the Roman kindergarten on the Gianicolo and the man buried prematurely in the cemetery of a distant city? A very intimate connection—the same person, the same child.

Very late on one learns that weakness isn't a defect in a person but a quality. A risky quality, which doesn't call for indulgence or severity but gratitude. The condition of a surviving parent is full of shame.

December

She's called Sofia—that is to say, Wisdom—a virtue human beings attribute to themselves but don't in the least possess. She was born on the third day of this month. She's Junior's great-niece, though he didn't live long enough to become a great-uncle.

Everyone regards this alternation of life and death as providential and poetic, a miracle of nature and the mystery of creation, a *perpetuum mobile* of earthly existence. But it's a philosophy full of hypocrisy.

Life goes on is an expression that is not just obvious but cynical, and the story never ends is cant. The reproduction and continuation of the species is an automatic process that conceals a kind of mockery. It's a breathless chase on a cylinder revolving in a void; it's the donkey that follows the carrot fixed to his nose.

Similar thoughts come and go under the medlar, like dark clouds. Bad thoughts. They aren't at all suited to the welcome Wisdom unreservedly merits.

Even the country house, where a strong winter wind is blowing, is inhabited by old fears. The end of the year freezes it in blocks of ice that summer won't be able to melt.

Experience isn't transmitted. It's a strictly private property that has no market, can't be bought or sold or exchanged, and can't be acquired in any way by alien customers. Putting yourself in someone else's shoes is an impossible exercise and a futile exhortation. Everyone keeps his own, even priests say *unicuique suum*.* Everyone is confined within impenetrable borders (monads without windows), like the three little monkeys that see no evil, hear no evil and speak no evil.

Don't say fortune is blind. She has excellent eyesight and amuses herself.

---

* To each his own.

1998

January

The names of the months are not without influence and that's why the Jacobins tried to change them, aiming to shatter a thousand-year-old tradition and inaugurate a different, enduring one. Revolutions entertain many illusions.

January owes its name to Janus,★ an untrustworthy, two-faced pagan divinity, to whom it was dedicated because it's advisable to curry favour with anyone who holds power by flattering them. He must have been much feared to deserve the first month in the calendar. That didn't change his character, though, and January remains the coldest month.

In the middle of the night, in the darkness of the room, ghosts, thieves and assassins arranged a meeting. They moved silently, brushing the floor or on tiptoe, but the creaking of the furniture revealed their presence. Giano held his breath and strained his ears to gauge their careful

---

★ *Giano*, like the name of the protagonist.

steps. The only solution was to huddle under the sheets, without leaving even a millimetre of his body exposed, not even a sliver of his skin. Especially the feet.

He didn't call them bad dreams but ugly dreams—a lexical difference only a child can grasp. His parents called them nightmares. Because you can't spend a whole night huddling under the sheets, it was necessary to find the courage to switch on the light and wait for the tall paternal figure to enter reassuringly in his long nightshirt.

One shouldn't forget the tremblings of childhood and one shouldn't guffaw at what children say, because they feel deeply humiliated by it.

In the crowded cinema, watching the wanderings of Ulysses and his final encounter with his old dog at home, the boy muttered a Homeric verse: 'half destroyed with flies, / Old Argos lay.'* His older friends laughed loudly, silencing him. A minute later, he marched from his seat, groped his way through the darkness of the auditorium and fled, silently weeping.

It is said that working through a bereavement requires two years. It's an unpleasant cliché, a formula from a manual of psychoanalysis, and an affected way of saying that time is a great healer—another cliché. Time can be an implacable enemy, a tormentor that turns wounds gangrenous instead of healing them. What's more, Giano is of such an age that there's no time or way to work through anything.

---

* Homer, *The Odyssey*, Book 17.

And why should it be necessary to work through a bereavement, as if it were an undigested meal to ruminate? Better to suppress it, if you're clever. Pablo's dead, who was Pablo?

There are things that can't be thought or said or written. The conviction, for example, of being close to death (a few weeks or some months or a day). Is it a warranted belief or a state of mind? The so-called exact sciences can provide an answer if there's proof of a serious illness but they can't if it's a malaise that does its work noiselessly and indirectly. A good cure—the best in fact—is to sleep fifteen hours out of every twenty-four.

Dogs look browbeaten even when no one beats them. That's why some people like them and some people don't. Inferring the character of a person from whether they prefer dogs or cats or neither is an interesting exercise, like inferring their cultural formation from whether they prefer Verdi or Wagner or neither.

Beat the drowning dog is a saying that doesn't speak well for the Chinese. The advice to sit on the riverbank and wait for the enemy's body to float by is also macabre. They're variations on the same theme.

'There is a street in Trieste where I see myself mirrored in long days of closed sadness, via del Casaletto Vecchio.'* Junior didn't like living there, even if he had the sea close by. Those verses by one of the city's poets, engraved on a slab of marble, prove him right.

It was a massive building, with old walls blackened by age and neglect. The rooms over the courtyard were also dark but spacious, and could offer hospitality to friends and conquer solitude. Faulty reasoning, because solitude isn't a material thing and doesn't have friends.

By contrast, the Lutheran cemetery is small and bright. There was a sudden downpour. Perhaps it was a deliberate welcome or perhaps the opposite; it's difficult to interpret heavenly signs. Giano observes the swaying cypresses and asks himself if they're sad because they're in the cemetery, or if they're in the cemetery because they're sad. It's an unanswerable question.

A young English princess has died in a car crash and there's been a lot of public emotion. A nun of Indian adoption has

---

* The misremembered first line of Umberto Saba's poem 'Tre Vie', which speaks of Via del Lazzaretto Vecchio.

died of old age and there's been a lot of public emotion. More for the first than the second, on account of age and status. Who knows why important corpses are displayed on gun carriages, which evoke anything but pity and peace.

Emotion seizes hold of great crowds when it costs nothing; it doesn't involve responsibility and is devoid of consequences. The death of a celebrity is impersonal and symbolic; people throng behind the crush barriers and the military cordons and can throw flowers and shed tears at the sight of a funeral procession with no further cares. They aren't bitter tears but comforting ones. Then we feel light, as at the end of a feast on a Sunday in spring.

It isn't so simple if you run into an emaciated child on a street corner or you're shown a column of outcasts in the wastes of some continent. The message they convey is threatening—emotion is dangerous, repression is automatic.

Social stratification between countries, strata and individuals in the shape of luxury and misery (wealth and poverty, domination and servitude, superiority and inferiority, etc.) is once again regarded as physiological and required by a healthy economy. As a result, evangelical and seigneurial charity is being rehabilitated as a counterweight. Following the upheaval of the egalitarian revolutions and the inconclusiveness of redistributive exercises, the dominant philosophy is that of the ladies of San Vincenzo who volunteer to serve breakfast in soup kitchens on Sundays. Even the governors of central banks like to be photographed throwing a coin into an old person's bowl on the steps of a church.

It's better to do it out of kindness, confidentially. There was a fellow who didn't frequent charitable venues who nevertheless couldn't meet a beggar on the street without greeting him and giving him loose change, fishing it out of his waistcoat with two fingers. If it was a phoney—someone feigning blindness, a pretend cripple, a trained little tramp—he thought they merited the offering for their performance.

Spring is approaching and it's time to have done with complaints and maintain with the utmost firmness that the world is proceeding for the best. Why vilify the horsemen of the Apocalypse? War, famine, disease, death and all the rest (there are more than four horsemen)—what's so calamitous about them? They're ways of being and, as such, are to be faced manfully and perhaps even kindly welcomed.

Life is struggle and struggle is life is a play on words, but for many it's a revolutionary principle and a good thing. Might as well believe it's true and bravely desire to live one day as a lion rather than a week as a sheep.* The pirates' and fascists' idea of displaying a skull and crossbones as an emblem is brilliant.

Beware of appearances. *Tanto va la gatta al lardo . . .* isn't, as one might think, an anti-feminist proverb.** Why *la gatta* and not *il gatto*? There's a scientific explanation—

---

* Gramsci used a variant of this proverb, which was also employed as a Fascist slogan, in his *Prison Notebooks* (1929–35).

** The English equivalent of the Italian proverb *Tanto va la gatta al lardo, che ci lascia lo zampino* (the cat goes to the lard so often that she forgets her paw) is 'curiosity killed the cat'. But the author's point would be lost in translation.

the female cat is more ravenous when she's suckling her offspring and consequently runs more risks. There's also a musical explanation; there's no rhythm to *tanto va il gatto al lardo*.

Totalitarianism and democracy are two words without qualities. They would need several adjectives precisely in order to qualify them. A despotism can be enlightened and a democracy rotten; and it isn't easy to disentangle oneself from these antinomies.

A seasoned animal-rights activist, or even Aesop, might say that the difference between these two forms of power consists in the fact that the first traps you in a cage with closely spaced bars, like big cats in zoos, whereas the second confines you in an airy enclosure where you can wander round, like camels and giraffes. It too is a privation of freedom but it's much more intelligent and those who suffer it don't even notice.

To have reduced the revolutions of the twentieth century to a pile of horrors is a Manichaean operation in the strict sense. If that is evil, everything else is good and the world can feel itself to be ultimately innocent. A half-rotten, half-fresh watermelon, to be served sliced in two. No one suspects that the implosion of these revolutions didn't betoken the defeat of one side and the salvation of the other, but a missed opportunity for everyone and an inauspicious sign for the whole watermelon.

Historians, journalists, black books and colourful documents insist that the most recent revolutions cost eighty-five million lives, which comes to almost a million a year over the course of a century. Double the Second World War, which in fact managed to concentrate its deaths into six years. And since Giano sided heartily with those revolutions, he feels guilty. Unfortunately, any slave revolt, from Spartacus onwards, has the power to seduce him despite the cost and futility of the undertaking.

In the event, he finds the tally partial and considers himself the guilty heir of something much worse. Where, once a year, Voltaire lit a candle and placed it in his window so as not to forget the Saint Bartholomew's Day massacre, Giano would need a many-branched candelabrum and a wide balcony to honour the charnel houses on which modern states are built.

A meticulous bookkeeper has calculated that, during the First World War, eleven thousand men died every day for four years—illiterate soldiers and young officers, few civilians, without weapons of mass destruction, with bayonets fixed to rifles, machine guns with belts, helmets and puttees, behind sandbags and coils of barbed wire, under the fireworks of howitzers and hand grenades.

Military cemeteries are more numerous in the European countryside than Gothic churches in cities; and there isn't a village without a hierarchical list of lieutenants, sergeants, corporals and privates fallen while serving their country. Yet at that time there were only ruling dynasties, bourgeoisie and plebs. Communism was a philosophical manifesto for a very restricted circle. That war is by far the best key for interpreting the history of the last two centuries.

No doubt the largest candle, like the trunk of a redwood, is for the Jews massacred in the most cultured country in the world. The second in order of size (however difficult it is to establish a hierarchy in this matter) goes to the atomic bomb on Nagasaki. Not the one on Hiroshima, the first, but the one on Nagasaki, the second. A crime in its purest state, testing out a single crematorium on the population of a whole termitary, a bequest to future humanity.

It wasn't referred to at Nuremberg; it wasn't appropriate. Who knows today, so long afterwards, what the world would say if a bomb like that had been dropped on Hamburg by a Soviet pilot the day before the war ended? But he didn't have it and so they all trudged on foot to Berlin.

That's perhaps why the Sphynx-like image of Stalin still looms large in the collective imaginary, and Stalinist is a defamatory political adjective. Those who venerated him can't forgive him for having violated the revolution; those who opposed him can't forgive him for having won the war. That patriarchal photo of the three victors on a terrace in Crimea, relaxed on antiquated wicker chairs, is in comic contrast with the posthumous demolition of the dictator.

Russia and China inspired a fear in the developed world it had never previously experienced (perhaps Europe with Napoleon or Rome with the barbarian invasions). Not because they possessed an impenetrable regime or a bellicose disposition but because, in the eyes of much of humanity, they made an attempt on the life of an age-old property structure and promised redress. The West knows from experience that the wealth of nations is mixed with blood and tears and it isn't this detail that made Stalin a mortal enemy. It was a question of improper competition.

That competition was excessively ambitious, given that America is unbeatable on its home ground. It was created out of a genocide in the literal sense, by a ferocious civil war between usurping colonists, by a lethal Biblical morality. And from this genealogy and tradition, which includes the colt revolver as a character trait, it has fashioned an epic and derived maximum glory. For this it's the most envied and admired of all countries. Who says that the end, when it reaches as high as skyscrapers, doesn't justify the means?

Only the Roman Catholic Church merits equivalent recognition—greater even, considering its longevity. It hasn't lost its sacredness and reverence while proving capable of phenomenal cruelties; and it successfully preaches humility while being the most opulent of earthly organizations (the celestial ones aren't known but Dante's *Paradiso* is extremely rich in special effects and psychedelic suggestions). The impunity of the Roman Church, and of its witchcraft in competition with modern technology, is ultimately proof of its supernatural origin.

Even so, Giano continues to think that the world is too populous to be governed by a single sovereign and that the watermelon is fated to roll like any round thing. Even in geography there are antipodes and the four points of the compass and geopolitics can't escape this rule.

It's impressive how many keys, cards and forms one uses in daily life. A utopian communism, which is better than the scientific variety, might be a world without keys.

April

Again and again, however we know the landscape of love
and the little churchyard there, with its sorrowing names.
. . . again and again the two of us walk out together under
the ancient trees, lie down again and again among the
flowers, face to face with the sky.*

Even the reproduction of the species can be translated
into poetry.

A spring rain is falling, but the legal hour** is illegal and
injurious to the rhythm of the seasons.

An unexpected fainting fit. He falls like skittles, without
warning. Never happened before. The fault of a drug
prescribed in huge doses. Which is more dangerous—a bad
doctor, a bad judge or a bad priest? Difficult question,
because all three, to varying degrees, possess the power of

---

* Rainer Maria Rilke, 'Again and Again'. Without quotation
marks in the original.

** *L'ora legale* or Daylight Saving Time.

life and death. One by virtue of a degree and a white coat; one by virtue of an examination and a gown; and one by virtue of a vocation and a cassock.

His final thought before fainting was that circumflex brackets definitely exist, even if they're rarely used. There are those who deny their existence and confuse them with the circumflex accent, which is also rare in modern languages. And even the dictionary doesn't refer to circumflex brackets; it uses the term 'brace' instead, more appropriate to a metal worker than a philologist. It's necessary to hold on to some certainty, to have the courage of one's convictions to the end, to take it as read that circumflex brackets exist.

He smokes more than the usual six cigarettes an hour and wonders indiscriminately about brackets, the conduct of the democracies in the Spanish Civil War and the etymology of the word *marameo*.* All of a sudden he remembers that egg white and cream in his milk used to make him vomit and would like to understand the reasons for these childish idiosyncrasies—deglutition or psychology? If he eats trout, he asks how such a sophisticated organism can serve as food and be reduced to an intake of calories or even thinks of one of Schubert's six hundred lieder, which is called 'The Trout'. In short, he can't eat a trout in peace.

---

* As in the expression *fare marameo a . . .*, to thumb one's nose or cock a snook at.

It's curious that the figurative arts don't treat eggs with the respect they deserve. One can walk through the rooms of a major museum without finding a still life with eggs. Vegetables predominate by far. Yet their form is perfect and, like bottles, readily lends itself to an infinite variety of compositions.

It's also curious that bipeds, quadrupeds and millipedes exist in nature, but not tripods. Yet three-legged tables are perfectly stable and stability is something also much appreciated in politics.

May

May is a cherished month, but the origin of its name is disputed. It's not a good idea to use words when you don't know their meaning.

When Maria M., my grandmother's housekeeper, died, funerals weren't hole-and-corner affairs as they are now. They still crossed the city with relatives and friends behind the hearse, on foot or in cars, and were more or less crowded depending on the social status of the deceased. Giano remembers that people would stop on the pavement out of compunction, raise their hat and make the sign of the cross.

As a young person, accompanying Maria M., who had died of asthma, Giano thought two things: that she had lived completely toothless, because Grandmother never bought her dentures; and that her *castagnacci* and *buccellati** were unrivalled anywhere in the world. It was an injustice that bystanders didn't know all this; that the newspapers hadn't mentioned it; and that Maria M. didn't have a gravestone in Spoon River.

---

* Traditional sweets.

Although from a poor background, Maria M. had kept a trousseau of valuable fabrics in a trunk. During the war, she traded it on the black market to obtain white flour, oil, sugar and other foodstuffs from the local shopkeepers. The buckeye flour came directly from Lucchesia, her birthplace. She had a daughter whom she was always talking about but who was never there, and so she transferred her maternal instinct to the grandchildren of her miserly mistress. As grown-ups, would these grandchildren have reciprocated Maria M.'s love with a set of dentures? Not necessarily; the general opinion was that she got on perfectly well without them. She was a beautiful old woman, with very straight posture, naturally dressed in black or at most grey. Her perfectly ironed white aprons made her stand out.

She was naturally amiable and continued to be so even when asthma reduced her breathing to a wheeze. Right up to the end, she continued to accompany her mistress, bereft of sight and mentally adrift, in a social round between the bedroom walls. Grandmother dressed with great pomp and looked at the windows of imaginary shops, convinced she was walking the main roads of the city between the coffee tables of her youth.

She was affable with children and won the sympathy of Giano's friends, trading her anti-asthma cigarettes with them in contraband. A precious commodity to be found in pharmacies, now that the tobacconists' shelves were at war like the whole nation. The humble are often generous to the point of sharing their oxygen cylinder.

Every once in a while the pain sinks to the depths, then resurfaces through a chance, powerful stimulus, and then returns from whence it came. It goes up and down but doesn't change, either when it comes to the surface or when it descends to the depths. It's worth repeating that time isn't a skilful physician but a meticulous tormentor, it doesn't heal but infects.

Yet knowledge of pain isn't amenable to being encapsulated in a formula. No one really knows where the ill is centred, whether in the brain like a rodent, in the lungs like a pressure point, in the heart (a favourite place) like a blade, in the blood like a poison, or in every fibre like a shiver. But this is a macabre list, pointlessly verbose. Perhaps pain is merely darkness.

Many friends urge Giano to react on the assumption (Senior*) that 'action is escaping solitude'. But one would need to know what action.

---

* Throughout Senior refers to Giaime Pintor (1919–43), Luigi's elder brother; and Junior to his son, Giaime Pintor (1950–97).

June

What is there to do in the course of a day? Take a shower, possibly pay an old bill, make telephone calls, drink numerous coffees and a glass of alcohol in the evening, go two hundred metres on foot and get on a bus to come back.

These habits aren't actions, not even activities. Acting would mean inciting, influencing, changing. If action has no impact, and doesn't create anything new, it's a mask for inertia.

In the city, Giano doesn't come upon anything new. With his eyes closed he can do five different walks from house to church; he knows every corner and every door, every sign and every window. Rain or shine, it makes little difference; even the pedlars and beggars are always the same. He can take a detour via a public garden but doesn't rediscover the air of his childhood.

He can meet up with people but doesn't know who and where; few like speaking honestly and his conversation is off-putting. He can go on an outing but it isn't in fashion and wouldn't distract him; even in the environs everything is similar and his thoughts don't change. He can listen to music but knows that the ringing of the telephone is enough to put him off.

Even those who shave on alternate days repeat the operation twelve thousand times in the course of an average lifetime.

Doing scales and arpeggios on the piano, playing chess with the computer, putting things down in black and white—these aren't actions but pastimes. Not having a goal would at least demand perfection. Scarlatti's sonatas are meaningless if the performance isn't crystalline.

Giano is nostalgic for the past with a small p more than for the one with a capital P—for example, tailors' shops, haberdasheries, resoled shoes. It's not for nothing that tailors and cobblers feature in many tales and fairy stories. And, fortunately, there are enduring objects that challenge time and valiantly compete with modernity. Scissors, for example, elegant and ingenious. Buttons and button-holes—an inconvenient invention no zip has proved capable of dethroning. Shoelaces, which counsel patience.

He has misplaced nostalgia even for the newspaper of the Italian Communists. When as a young man he worked on it devotedly, he couldn't imagine how that noble masthead could ever have anything in common with a Dutch finance company. History with a capital H (the major downfalls) is no laughing matter, but history with a small h (the minor degenerations) is funny. Those who produced that paper underground risked their skin; even in freedom many people gave their all for it, as if the fate of the world depended on it. They didn't think it would end up being auctioned off.

Back then, Italian Communist leaders were stern characters who didn't get familiar, kept people in awe, enjoyed a kind of monopoly rent and made it count because they could allow themselves to. The best were the least well known, humbly working in obscurity. But they all seriously believed in what they were doing, unlike their descendants, and were certain that the wheel of history was turning in their favour.

To paint them in a good light, it's common today to regard them as a national peculiarity. But to separate the personnel and fortunes of Italian Communism from the international setting they operated in is stupid. The Comintern was something more serious and less abstruse than its acronym. It wasn't a satanic sect, a masonic lodge, a society of Carbonari, a Red Brigades hideout or a deviant secret service. And it's a pity one can't browse round in that maze without running up against historical and anti-historical stereotypes.

A nursery for naughty children. Giano isn't clear what this refers to, but he has the impression that he's attended many of them in his life, in every latitude.

July

A year has passed under the medlar tree, but that's not true. Calendars, like clocks, lie.

The poet asks why it is that every animal is content to laze about, but 'if I ever lie down to rest, boredom invades my breast'.* Apparently, even for a poet well practised in gazing at the moon, contemplation is no easier than action. Yet it isn't boredom that assails Giano—not even solitude. In good weather, glow-worms, thought to be extinct,** dot the night with mysterious delicacy and keep one company.

Freedom and equality too are words without qualities and stepsisters that don't get on. Those who've tried to com-bine them since the world began, philosophers and

---

* Giacomo Leopardi, 'Night Song of a Wandering Shepherd in Asia'.

** A reference to Pasolini, for whom the disappearance of glow-worms was an allegory for the extinction of pre-industrial Italy and its ways of life. See 'Il vuoto del potere', *Scritti Corsari* (1 February 1975).

revolutionaries of every school, have met with complete failure.

Freedom (you can do as you please) is favoured, like Cinderella's elder sisters, and can be achieved by some people for a time; equality (you can't do as you please) never. This is an inconvenient truth which two friends, neither philosophers nor revolutionaries, ascertained in experimental fashion in fortuitous circumstances.

One was an old printer, the other a young student. It fell to them to spend three days and three nights together in a toilet four metres square being used as a cell. And they felt equal and fraternal. Having happily regained their freedom, they met in the street, embraced with emotion, recalled their adventure and toasted their lucky escape. But to their great amazement they soon realized that they were no longer equal like they'd thought. Now the printer was an unemployed man who did house painting and the student lived in a house that was properly whitewashed.

Maybe at night, when you can't get to sleep, even television can placate. An Asian girl, sold as a child to a brothel and ill with AIDS in its final stages, calmly tells her story. She says she's a Buddhist but doesn't believe in reincarnation. She thinks there's no afterlife and makes it clear that, if it existed and was offered her, she'd refuse it. She's accumulated sufferings for which reparation can't be made, either in this life or a different one; and she doesn't want to know anything more about it. She explains that she doesn't kill herself because she has a little brother whom she'll look after for as long as she can.

Buddhists also hold a fascination for the West that Mohammedans don't. *Maometto** is a name translated without respect, which sounds disreputable for a messiah. And in the West all that is known about this character is that he went to the mountain if the mountain didn't come to him. *Maometto* sounds the same as Pinocchio and one can very well imagine him dressed in paper, in lines rather than flowers, in short breeches.

An Asian on a plane takes off his shoes and puts his feet up on the back of the seat opposite. An American might also do this. But this travelling companion is distinct from any other because he displays green socks with five toes, as if they were gloves. His feet look like the palms of a frog. The flight attendant is impressed and at the airport shop asks for socks with five toes. The cosmopolitan saleswoman is nevertheless baffled and maintains they don't exist (try a city store or even Japan, she cuts him short). But one can't go to Tokyo or Kyoto for an articulated sock, just as one can't go to Beijing for an ivory cigarette holder.

One shouldn't call someone a dotard, which is disrespectful. One should say he's become infantile, which is more precise.**

---

* The Italian form of Mohammed. The ending makes it sound like a diminutive, and hence derogatory.

** Untranslatable wordplay on *rimbambito* and *rimbambinito*, which plays on *bambino*, child or infant, linking senility with regression to childhood.

August

The first of August many years ago wasn't a day like any other for Giano. It began pleasantly with an excursion to the sea with his daughter Beba, his two-year-old firstborn. But that's not how it ended.

You had to take a train full of excited children and busy parents in the scorching heat to reach that coal-ridden coast. Where had the African beaches of his childhood gone? But the child scampered and entertained him, while the mother was in a Roman clinic expecting the birth of another assumed to be male and hence the inheritor of the family fortune.

When, at midday, he returned to the city and punctually entered the clinic's maternity ward, he was in for a surprise. The birth was proving difficult; the second child didn't want to come into the world and there was a danger to his life and the mother's. If it came to it, which of them should be sacrificed? The dazed parents responded by holding hands without noticing the effrontery of the question, the shady undertones of the dilemma—why was a second delivery difficult after a normal pregnancy? Why had an event that was unproblematic just an hour earlier taken a tragic turn?

They used forceps, like in the time of Giano's grandfather, and Junior emerged shrieking loudly but seemingly without complications. Thirty years later, the X-rays would show lesions across the cranial bones.

On a health record there's a stamp—subject to risk. A curt way of saying that death can occur at any time. But it's not nice to write it on a record in indelible ink, like a tattoo on the arm of a deportee. We're all subject to risk but kindly wish one another a long life.

Many of Trieste's streets are dedicated to young and very young people who died in war. If you walk with your eyes raised, you can read many plaques with names, military ranks and decorations, alpha and omega. The one who dies for his country is a subject at risk who can always count on a plaque. It's inscribed on it in invisible ink that human beings will not leave pre-history behind them as long as they go obediently to their death.

But hadn't we decided to have done with complaints and to change the subject?

A serial novel published in fortnightly instalments in the thirties is the only book Giano has read in its entirety. It was called *The Three Boy Scouts* and even the young Sartre confessed he'd read it voraciously.* It was interminable,

---

* The author of *The Three Boy Scouts* is Jean de La Hire.

vaguely colonialist but highly imaginative, with illustrated covers like the weeklies of the era, from the Pampas via the Sahara to the North Pole. It featured a gang led by a Red Devil and a faithful Eritrean Askari, who was called Zomba and intervened decisively at the last minute (like the negro Lothar with Mandrake).* Strangely, one of the three heroes was Swiss, perhaps because the French author didn't want a German getting in the way. The other two were French and Italian. Giano is probably the sole surviving reader.

For the rest, he was content with a children's encyclopaedia, perfect for a lazy reader like him dedicated to ignorance. It had the most beautiful illustrations, all the helmets and shields in history, all the instruments of torture down the centuries, a lot of games and numerous short stories and tales which always ended in the same way—narrow is the leaf, broad is the way.

By contrast, Senior devoured one book after another and recalls having read, between the ages of ten and fifteen, everything that had been written for children. He says this was the period when his culture was comparatively robust. He read very quickly and someone accused him of skipping pages. But it wasn't true. He could precisely recount all the adventures of the paladin Orlando and those of Astolfo on the moon,** Don Quixote's nag and even Till Eulenspiegel's pranks.

---

* *Mandrake* was a comic-book series started in the thirties, written by Lee Falk and then Phil Davis.

** Both characters from Ludovico Ariosto's sixteenth-century epic poem *Orlando Furioso*.

One morning his little brother caught him off guard, with his face lathered up, and asked him how it was possible to get good marks in Italian and mathematics at the same time. Senior cut himself with the razor and replied that doing well at school came more naturally to him than shaving. But he confessed he found it harder to write than it seemed to his friends and acquaintances.

Then Giano asked him if those two, Marx and Freud, whom people were secretly whispering about, deserved their reputation. He answered yes, but with the warning that no key fits all locks and one shouldn't believe in philosophers' stones. A precious warning that Giano didn't properly heed.

September

It's a very beautiful month with clear skies. The seasons defend themselves against the affronts of modernity and vigorously reassert their rights. But there's something funny in the air, something pending and menacing, a new foreboding. Yet everything has already taken place and nothing more can happen.

Today is Giano's birthday. So the impression of living on borrowed time wasn't justified. But it persists and, ultimately, a week or a month or a year makes no difference.

Birthdays can be counted backwards, going back to kindergarten. It was two steps away from the house, but to reach it one had to cross a square of puddles with annoying ankle boots the child couldn't put on. He didn't even know how to make paper boats or draw a daisy or a cat. But he has a clear memory of the teacher called Cochetta who later become a nun.

The elementary school was very poor and one of his schoolmates didn't wear shoes. The building was at the top of the city ramparts and school's out was festive. The teacher wore a red toupee to hide his baldness. But no one made fun of him, he was a genuine elementary-school teacher and often interrupted lessons to project Larry Semon's last silent comedies and Tom Mix's forays in an attic in an atmosphere of great enthusiasm.

The *ginnasio* teacher enforced discipline with nineteenth-century methods. He kept a long, flexible cane within reach on his desk and used it to tame the distracted or noisy pupils on the front benches. Or else he walked through the classroom gripping a different cane, short and sturdy, called zmaster Giorgio, which he administered on the hands of those who blotted their exercise books with ink. But he did it good-naturedly. He hated the Austrians and recounted episodes from the first war with passion (he said Austrians but it was 1935 and he meant to say Germans).

In the upper *ginnasio*, surprisingly, Giano came top of the class. This was thanks to the literature teacher, who took a liking to the undisciplined pupil, moved him up from the last bench and (to open his mind, he said) gave him a very difficult book on Emperor Augustus to read, in an orange colour edition that was very famous at the time. Flattered by the attention, Giano felt it his duty to reciprocate by learning Horace's *Ars Poetica*, including the prosody, by heart. Now he got nine in Latin and Greek but two in mathematics and French—a unique case of schizophrenia that made the final assessment and promotion to the *liceo* a drama.

In fact, he'd never have succeeded in passing the school certificate if the war and the American landing on the peninsula hadn't cancelled the exams. Yet he had excellent teachers who've been forgotten: a true Latinist with twelve sons in his charge who skipped to the rhythm of Horace's metrics; a philosophy teacher who read Averroes in Arabic; and a lover of Italian literature who was also an expert Germanist. It was a selective high school—that is common knowledge. But it was also a serious school—that was for sure. Giano regrets not having experienced it as a great opportunity and a great pleasure.

University was a different matter and disappointed him from the day he set foot in it. They'd told him that, during the war, the best university for some was prison or internment and that to do a degree now was a sign of conformism. Perhaps that was why the only academic exam he took was on Tiberius Gracchus' agrarian reform.

It's pointless escaping into the past if the present doesn't give you any peace. Wasn't this a year in which nothing bad could happen?

November

Beba died in the early hours of yesterday morning, 24 November. She was born on a summer's day to the sound of the noontime bells. She had had a short life and a terrible death. Evil (god? nature?) has an unlimited imagination.

It happened in a short space of time and with the fury of a hurricane, a year after her brother's death and twenty after her mother's. Of Giano's little family, formed after the war, there was no one left.

She was the first born, continuity, female memory. Her mother died after a long agony; her brother almost died by his own hand; she was violently snatched away. Evil has an unlimited imagination.

A confused diagnosis, a plethora of doctors, hit-and-miss treatment, much suffering. European Institute of Oncology. Nice name, glass hospital. But Hippocrates no longer lives there or anywhere else.

She wasn't in time to rail against death, which crept up on her unawares, but only against pain. She seemed transfigured, breathless, uncertain in her step and bewildered in her facial expression, with flashes of irony. Now the sister resembles her brother. The father wishes the illness on himself. At his age it wouldn't be a sacrifice but an opportunity. But such an exchange isn't permitted. Nothing is permitted. You can't be close to someone who is dying because they are absent, and you can't be distant from them because they are present.

There's time to take a stroll in the market square. Those who know her can scarcely conceal their astonishment at so abrupt a change in her appearance. She pauses on a bench to catch her breath, looks at the slides where the children are playing, bows her head and weeps in silence. But it's only a moment. Two months earlier, she'd brought Sapienza, who is less than a year old, to the seaside. They had big plans for the future.

'Dear Professor, please forgive this letter. I am writing it because I think my daughter is close to death, defenceless against both her illness and her suffering. The question I would like to ask you is this: Is there a way or place to die with dignity? Perhaps it is an inappropriate question. But does such a way or place exist?' It's a letter that was never sent.

The relatives of patients in large hospitals are foreigners. They hold their hat in their hands and look round with the silent question that you can read in dogs' eyes. No man of power has ever been in a casualty department or hospital ward. A culture of death doesn't exist, there isn't even a technique of death or a burial ritual. You go on a waiting list, as in airports or on ferries, whether you're buried or cremated.

Cremation in Western cultures has nothing purifying about it, as is possibly the case in other cultures. It's only a more efficient, less cumbersome, practice of burial which in turn isn't a return to the earth but a kind of cementation.

The crematorium in the Roman cemetery resembles an abandoned building site. Among the outdoor rubble were two forgotten coffins on wheeled trestles, waiting their turn. But there were also piles of dry flowers and that's how you know it isn't a building site.

In the family vault are seven boxes and two urns. It faces the sun. The stone with an elaborate inscription and blue mosaic has stood for ninety-eight years, repeatedly removed and replaced. Marble cutters were a serious guild.

Memory needs material references, things and places that feelings can attach to. That's why one reflects on tombs but more easily on a pile of bones than a pile of ashes.

What is the connection between the little girl who watched the kites on the beach at Ostia and the incinerated woman in that little urn? The same person, the same child. This absurdity exacerbates the grief.

'No one's irreplaceable and there is no void that can't be filled'—this assertion by Senior is decidedly secular but it's false or can only be true when you're twenty. Instead, you experience dizziness followed by fury. Everyday gestures become hateful; breathing and walking seem illegitimate. Abstaining from everything would be the only way to avoid persecution but you can't do it.

'Light open, door on.' That's how they said good night, switching the adjectives. That way it didn't seem like an abrupt separation between the big ones and the little ones, parents and children, and there remained a thread of communication even if the little ones went off to bed and the big ones went out. This ceremony was cheerful and trusting; light on and door open would have had no meaning. Now it's a past without witnesses.

'O clouds that cross the mountain and the plain, tell me, where are you going? Where is the wind taking you? I see you fly and with my hand wave farewell. But for you who am I?'

It's a poem written at ten years of age for a family celebration.

December

No one leads us through pastures green. If green pastures exist, we must walk through them alone.*

Beyond the darkened world that surrounds him, Giano can see expanses of grass damp with dew, lit by a tepid sun, white like the moon. The grass is scored with narrow tracks that branch in every direction and don't lead anywhere. His steps are slow and leave no trace. One advances brushing against the ground in light clothing and conversing with the air.

And yet it's difficult to imagine an immaterial world, a naked soul that has a life of its own, timeless and intangible. You can only intuit it, transparent and rarefied as in an aquarium, so slight and fragile it can't be offended.

These are the green pastures where Giano makes an appointment with his ghosts. It's an afternoon picnic, a tea on the lawn, where those present recount in happier spirits the things that happened in their life on earth—little

---

* Psalm 23.

games, surprises and disputes, understandings and farewells.

It's strange that Giano should think of green pastures, of which he has no experience, as opposed to a large, unconfined beach, with very fine sand, as white as the sun that warms it and then denser and darker at the sea's edge. This is his terrestrial experience and so it can't be transferred to a world of souls.

Our mind cannot know, or even conceive, anything beyond the bounds of matter. Beyond that, we cannot, by any conceivable effort, imagine a way of being, something different from nothing. We say that our soul is spirit. The tongue pronounces the name of this substance, but the mind can conceive no idea of it but this—that it does not know what, why and how it is. We shall imagine a wind, ether, a breath (and this was the first idea the ancients formed of the spirit, when they called it *pneuma* from *pneo* in Greek and *spiritus* from *spiro* in Latin). Among the Latins, soul too is taken for wind; we shall picture a flame; we shall pare down the idea of matter as much as possible to create for the likeness of an immaterial substance. But only a likeness; neither the imagination nor the thought of living beings can arrive at absence itself . . . inasmuch as, finally, it is the soul that cannot conceive itself (*Zibaldone*).*

---

* A collection of thoughts and aphorisms by Giacomo Leopardi.

172

It is possible to put into simple words the idea that human beings can envisage nothing outside of themselves and can conceive nothing that isn't on their own scale. That's why God has a large beard, angels are winged young boys, extraterrestrials are deformed humans or humanized machines and death a skeletal lady dressed in black.

Joy and sorrow are two ancient words that had a quality but have lost it. Growth and development are two words (one, in fact) without quality but that now exhaust our vocabulary. Modern society is like an individual whose model is obesity.

The evolutionary mechanism of the species, from its origins to extinction, wasn't determined by anyone in heaven or on earth. It's self-generating and fuels itself like a metastasis. It's self-destructive and will end in indigestion.

Religiosity is a request for reparation against this fate. But to trust established religions to find an answer is a dangerous gambit. The result is a bitter mixture of lordship and bondage—the pride of those who offer the chalice and the humility of those who drink from it; payment for officiating ministers and consolation for the churchgoing multitude.

Politics is a poor surrogate, a technique geared to debasing the ideals that nourish it, very far removed from those who put their trust in it. Yet it was the salt of the earth, and it isn't clear if it's the salt or the earth that's changed.

The expression of leaders in group photographs on the day they're sworn in. The joy of satisfied ambition, the parade of vanity. Their heartbeats under their full ceremonial dress should be counted. They experience that moment like a nuptial flight.

The petty leaders who are becoming fashionable in the West resemble one another like drops of water. They share an inconsistency that transpires from their guiltless faces. They have no mettle because they have no history and if they did they'd feel lost.

Judas is the symbol of betrayal. But he was merely a ham-fisted petty trader who sold a priceless commodity for a few coins (how much would thirty pieces of silver be in dollars?). A poor man who later hanged himself out of remorse.

A real traitor, by contrast, is calm when he takes his profits and if by his labours he manages to satisfy his *amour propre*, which, according to the hunchback of Recanati, is the mainspring of all human behaviour. Turning his coat isn't a vulgar adaptation to circumstances but a self-sublimation. And he doesn't hang himself.

It's very clear in the political sphere and in social relations. No one is more reactionary than a penitent revolutionary, than a worker who becomes a little boss, than someone who gets a taste of privilege after having suffered hardship. He changes himself completely—every gesture, not just his tie.

Giano wouldn't be able to say which of the last two years has been the worst. Perhaps the next one.

1999

January

These meanderings will make a bad impression on anyone who reads them after my death. In the form of maxims, sayings, aphorisms, epitaphs, epigrams, it was fashionable to print them on the strips of tissue paper that chocolates used to be wrapped in. Or else, in the form of astrological forecasts, they could be read on the multicoloured slips of paper that a trained parrot used to take out of a tray hung round a tramp's neck. It's not clear why this picturesque form of charity, which captivated children on street corners, is no longer in vogue.

The full light of the sun no longer penetrates the city. The vintage photographs that portray Roman streets and squares, palaces and fountains, are almost invariably summer ones and a glorious sun is striking the pavements and creeping into every crevice. Canvas awnings barely protect shop windows and the rare passers-by project a shadow.

People who walk hastily today don't have a shadow—the sun has no time to leave this trace—and the light doesn't reach the pavements but stops at the dirty roofs of cars. There's no need for canvas awnings.

It isn't a question of air pollution, poisonous gases or holes in the ozone layer. There's a denser filter that extinguishes the sun, a filter that bears not the least resemblance to the shady foliage of a medlar tree or a wood, an ultramodern filter fitted in people's minds to deprive them of their own shadow.

There's a tale about a man who loses his shadow and another about a man who loses his nose. But losing one's nose can be advantageous for some people (Cyrano, Pinocchio) whereas those who lose their shadow have no soul.

A census should be carried out of the slums and substrata of modern cities and Dante should be commissioned to map them. Novelists once devoted themselves to such explorations—Parisian sewers and London docks. Today, cinema uses them as material for science fiction.

The most interesting feature of the Moscow underground isn't the sumptuous mosaics or the ragged beggars that inhabit it, but the combination of the two, past pride and present humiliation. Primacy in fact goes to the substrata of American cities, as the flip side of that continent's gross domestic product.

Two sewage systems exist—one to channel organic waste, the other to dump social refuse.

The Roman Pope has declared that the computer has changed his life. The gadget instead of grace, the Internet instead of the communion of saints. It isn't true that *la farina del diavolo va in crusca.**

It's easy to read the Bible. You can find it in the bedside tables of hotels like bars of soap in the bathrooms. It's less easy to understand it.

The patience of Job is a common saying that doesn't do justice to the character. He was a tireless fighter, capable of standing up to his God who treated him like a wretch. But perhaps Junior wouldn't agree with this interpretation.

> Let the day perish wherein I was born, and the night in which it was said, There is a man child conceived. . . . Let that day be darkness. . . . Let darkness and the shadow of death stain it. . . . Lo, let that night be solitary, let no joyful voice come therein. . . . Because it shut not up the doors of my mother's womb, nor hid sorrow from mine eyes. Why died I not from the womb? (Job 3–11)

You need to be very sincere and free in spirit and heart to launch into such a fierce invective. Not in a moment of desperation and hatred but with lucid determination, not biting your tongue immediately afterwards, not being content with harbouring it in silence but shouting it out in front of everyone.

The string quartet is a perfect form. It's strange because they're homogeneous instruments and their interaction

---

* Literally, the devil's flour goes into the bran. The closest proverbial equivalent in English is 'no good comes from ill-gotten gains'.

should prove wanting. Instead, it encapsulates music in all its possible combinations.

No one wants to improve the world any more; they all want to make it wealthier and think that's the same thing. Get rich is the most widespread message and the one with the biggest audience. It's an incitement to criminality dignified by the Protestant ethic, encouraged by the double morality of Catholicism and protected to all intents and purposes by the law.

A pity Senior wasn't able to implement his plan for an intercontinental publishing house. In the post-war period, it could have been a portent of greater significance than the single currency.

One no longer says maimed but disabled or handicapped. Maimed is a word that refers to a person and his or her body—a child with crutches, a man with one arm, a crippled woman. It suggests war or an industrial accident or an individual mishap. Handicapped, by contrast, is an imported word that doesn't refer to a person but signals a reduced functionality and a category outside the parameters of productivity. It's a lexical variation that has nothing to do with philology and a lot to do with ideology. Even to say non-sighted and non-hearing, rather than blind and deaf, isn't a respectful way of expressing oneself but a socially reassuring artifice. Only the mute remain mute.

If Giano goes off in search of an old film transferred onto videocassette (excusing himself for the word), he doesn't find what he's looking for. He doesn't find Wallace Beery, for example, who in the golden age of American cinema was more than a character actor. He was Pancho Villa in the Mexican Revolution or the pirate in *Treasure Island* with a wooden leg and a parrot on his shoulder.

If he recalls this actor, it's because in the life of every child are moments that make their mark regardless of their actual significance. But one can't ask a producer of videocassettes to take account of them.

In films, Tarzan has long hair but no beard. There's no film of Tarzan with a beard. It's implausible that he had a razor in the jungle but no scissors for his hair. Anyhow, why should he have shaved? That he was hairless can also be ruled out; the monkeys wouldn't have taken to him.

High or low, big or small, ugly or beautiful and so on— these are conventional contrasts. Ultimately, everything is equivalent, with the exception of mine and yours, which children learn to distinguish in the first year of life.

Individuals are also equivalent, out of inconsistency. They come into the world on a courtesy visit and rapidly return where they dwelled before being born—that is, nowhere and outside time. The mystery doesn't lie elsewhere but in this parenthesis opened between two nothings, organic life as a freak of the universe.

When one sees the world in this sinister light, the best thing is to invent a different one and talk with ghosts. Many madmen behave thus and some seem at peace with themselves. But ghosts don't willingly lend themselves to this game and, as a general rule, they don't talk back.

March

These days people are playing heads or tails to know if a war will break out in the Balkan peninsula. Its coasts are very popular in high season and travel agents are worried.

By contrast, the war is looked on favourably by leaders of every stamp and with indifference by the public mind, because it won't be dangerous. It will be fought twenty against one and is forecast to be humanitarian since it will only cause casualties on one side. Excluding 'holy' wars, it's the most bizarre adjective that has ever been applied to an armed conflict.

It's not nice to stay under a medlar tree and keep a diary or monthly account when the carnival's in full swing.

People can't abide sharing a common lot and every individual regards him- or herself as an exception. The nose isn't a protuberance everyone has on their face, variously shaped but with two nostrils. Every individual likes to think their own nose is a unique detail and cares for it enormously. The idea of equality is completely foreign to human beings, whether in little things or big ones. That's why even war is regarded as someone else's business until it comes knocking at the door.

There are crafts that have disappeared through exhaustion, while others have gone as a result of inflation. For example, laundresses pertain to the first category and jesters or clowns to the second.

The latter was a clearly recognized craft when it was practised in courts or circuses and made people laugh by contrast with strict manners and normal conduct. Now even the serious people who appear on TV are used to posing in this way, especially in political talk shows but also in academic debates and, on the most diverse occasions, even when commenting on a bombing or taking part in a military funeral. The difference is that it's not funny.

In Paris, a Catholic philosopher of the French Academy has died, proclaiming himself certain in his will that humanity is visibly progressing and that a child in the year 2000 will enjoy a superior, more adoring life (he used precisely that phrase).

In Rome, the mayoralty has affixed a poster to litter bins with the head of a child coming out of another miniature bin, as in a game of Russian dolls, which addresses this adoring plea to passers-by: I'm a child, take me to a hospital or a safe place.

Catholic and French academician is an unbeatable combination.

It's a spring morning and the passer-by, having reflected on the litter bin's moral, crosses the square under a pale sun to be reconciled with the world. A fishmonger's advertises heart shapes of cod depicted in red varnish for sale. Are they really cod hearts or affectionately described choice morsels? The passer-by gives up on becoming reconciled with the world.

A stone in a little cemetery recalls two brothers, who died young in 1899 within twenty days of one another. And a third brother who likewise died young, in 1912. Obviously, the parents had persevered, meeting with the same misfortune thirteen years on. The weird thing is that on the back of the stone are many other names and surnames, but not those of the parents, who've vanished into thin air. Not that they didn't have good reasons to vanish.

Giano would like the children back, to talk to them, to start from the beginning. But having people back isn't allowed and so he'd like to wash his memory out, like you wash out a glass. But an ecology of the mind is impracticable, like the art of living—they're two titles for books which, like any good book, are useless.

June

Sure enough, the war broke out, provided a spectacle for two months and ended in the same way as a seasonal blossoming. It will come again without cause or purpose like the Trojan War, hatched by the bored inhabitants of Olympus.

Consequently, the flavour of summer has changed. It's no longer the season of heavy atmospheres and noiseless dawns but of Biblical exoduses. It isn't unruffled but frantic, and cries out for rain to wash it clean. It's not so much in itself that war is evil but because of the marks it leaves behind and the deep wounds that it carves.

Mass graves are a consequence of war or a consequence of poverty. The former are less numerous but enjoy greater notoriety. The latter are generally overlooked.

Even when it comes to the deceased, they'd all prefer to be on their own or in the company of relatives. But it's a mistake because, on the day of judgement and resurrection anonymous, crowded graves will have to take precedence since the last shall be first.

Who knows if Pasqualina, who came to do the washing once or twice a week, is at rest in a mass grave. People used to say 'do the washing' [*fare il bucato*] when laundry was still washed by hand. A strange phrase, derived perhaps from *bucon*, which in lingua franca means immersion.

She was a small, middle-aged woman, a widow without relatives, skinny and grumpy but actually very strong, judging from the way she wrung the laundry. She washed it in a big terracotta bowl and hung it out in the garden to dry.

The bowl [*conca*] was imposing and for that reason was familiarly called *concone*. Giano had to stand on tiptoe to look inside it, or hoist himself up with his arms over the rim. She used the *concone* for work while he used it for play, manoeuvring underwater bottles with a complex mechanism of weights and counter-weights. Until he fell in.

Those two rooms at the bottom of the garden where the *concone* had pride of place were called the country kitchen. There was nothing but folding tables and a battery of coal stoves built into the wall. One could play football against the walls without doing any damage and without having to account to anyone—an excellent pastime on rainy days when Pasqualina didn't do the washing because she couldn't hang the laundry in the garden.

In the last two months, Giano has interrupted these fantasies and given up playing against the walls with his memory. For forty days he has returned to his old craft and written twenty-five times against the spring bombing campaign. But he has the impression of having continued to do the same thing with the same results. Words too bounce off the walls.

July

In the sunny clearing there is a single tree. The sheaves of straw are scorching, like in the canvases of the mad painter.* The sheep crowd together in a patch of shade. Everyone needs a shady patch to take refuge in.

On the edge of the wood there's a sign—respect the nests of the red ants, which protect the plants against parasites. But nothing can be done about loggers.

Who was Mido? A country labourer who during his life, from the time he was ten years old to the day before he fell ill, built many homes, painted many walls, pruned many olive trees and cut a lot of grass. He had a meagre pension, his employers regularly ripped him off even when he worked on construction sites, and at the end he earned ten thousand lire an hour and was a stickler for precision. In his village, he had a dwelling with two rooms that has been put up for auction along with the shed where he kept two dogs. He has left a trace on every stone, lawn and wood in the environs. He too deserves a grave in Spoon River.

---

* Vincent van Gogh.

At the funeral, there were many people from the neighbouring villages, who filed in procession from the church to the cemetery. Mido was a good friend and in their hearts everyone was in his debt. But his more immediate fellow countrymen weren't there. When his home went up for auction, they remained indifferent. He'd stopped playing cards with them and spent his evenings alone in his clean, tidy kitchen.

At the end, his body had shrunk; on his bed, it seemed as if he was an empty pair of pyjamas. Yet three months earlier he'd climbed like a cat onto the cherry trees to hang coloured scarecrows on the highest branches.

'Whoever has power for a minute commits a crime.'* A highly intelligent observation.

Left is a conventional term that it would be advisable to remove from political terminology and restore to toponymy. Where's the exit? At the back on the left. On the third day, he rose from the dead and ascended to Heaven, where he is seated at the right hand of the Father . . . In its political sense it must be a couple of centuries old, with parliamentary origins in physical location in assemblies. Like the south stand in football stadiums.**

Perhaps it was intended to indicate an asymmetry. Essentially, a left-hander is an outsider with respect to customs; otherness is associated with criticism, alluding not to an equilibrium but an imbalance and upheaval

---

* Anne Michaels, *Fugitive Pieces* (1996).

** The *curva sud* is the term generally used in Italy for that section of the stadium occupied by the hard-core supporters, or *ultras*.

(revolution is a word that is also to be restored to astronomy). For this reason it's a location incompatible with power and, when it attains it, it creates a short circuit and commits its crime.

If Brother Francis had been summoned by Innocent III to govern Rome, he would have hung on for twenty hours, rather than one minute, before committing his crime. But then he would have had no choice. Either return post haste to Assisi to tame the wolf or become a wolf in his turn.

Why aren't people taught to write with both hands? At the piano it requires a lot of extra application to bring the left hand up to the level of the right, until they are indistinguishable. It's strange that the violin, and every string instrument, is constructed in such a way as to engage the weaker hand and fingers acrobatically.

Marxists don't understand women (Senior). Marxists don't understand people (Anonymous).

At the end of this month Beba would have turned fifty-two. Like a year ago, she'd be on a beach on the island of the Moors. Photographs capture her playing with Sapienza. The house at the seaside didn't have a phone and the father sent his best wishes by telegram. This year he'd use a mobile to know if all was well.

'Narrow is the leaf, broad is the way; tell yours, for I have told mine.' The child didn't understand the meaning of this chant and this moral, which rounded off fairy tales. Now he supposes that *foglia* stands for sheet or page, a trifle compared with the great, terrible world, a pebble on the motorway. So let everyone say their peace and recount what they can, sitting on a curbstone.

August

Two years (seven hundred and thirty days) have passed since Giano sat himself down. But it isn't true; calendars lie like clocks. This thesis, already stated, has been verified countless times and proved by the fact that the October Revolution used to be celebrated in November.

At this point, the sheet could expand to infinity, like an encyclopaedia. But that would be contradictory, because Giano's ambition is a silence he isn't capable of.

The metaphor of the moth is hackneyed but eloquent, and fires the imagination more than the myth of Icarus or Prometheus. The moth isn't mythological but exists in nature. It reacts as a result of a mechanism that entomologists can observe up close when it buzzes madly round the lamp until it burns its fragile wings and falls to the ground, incinerated. It's a fatal attraction, an ecstasy, a desire for death, similar to the passions that blind man, the desires he wants to satisfy at any cost, the mysteries he wants to penetrate regardless of the risks. Even knowing the disproportionately high price and suicidal outcome, it seems the lamp is worth the game. Weapons and exploits, power, wealth, progress, but also *amour propre* and hatred of the other, pride, a taste for rivalry—these are all invincible drives that prompt men and butterflies to spread their giddy wings.

At the foot of the mountain, where there aren't medlars but apple trees, it's possible to peek through the foliage at the clouds and kites flying. Children run in the field looking behind them to see if the kite is catching the wind and tumble over roughly. Old men entertain themselves while pretending to entertain their grandchildren. The kite is joyful when it flaunts its colours and quivers impatiently in the air.

They used to be made of tissue paper with a cane frame, almost all in the shape of a rhombus, more like a flat fish than a winged creature. They were more difficult to control; there was an imbalance and contest between the weight of the frame and the fragility of the paper. Now they're uglified but functional, as progress demands.

It's not worth the effort, especially at night, to climb onto an unstable chair to change a blown light bulb. You can slip, lose your balance and break five ribs in free fall.

What is to be done? It's a historical question to which, as a general rule, there is no answer. You find yourself in the pitch black, flat and immobile on the floor. You can't screech like a hen, whimper like a dog, squeak like a mouse, creep like a worm. *Little Man, What Now?* A fine novel by a writer now forgotten because fortune is fickle. With this thought he falls asleep. It can't even be said of a blown bulb that it does no one any harm.

'The outcome of human actions is something other than what the agents aim at and actually achieve, something other than what they immediately know and will.' A quotation from Hegel* lifted from a novel on a Venetian conspiracy of 1310 that ended badly. It applies to major collective events but also to individual affairs; and it applies to everyone, be they a revolutionary or an electrician.

---

* Georg Wilhelm Friedrich Hegel, *Lectures on the Philosophy of History* (1837).

September

There's another small indigenous war underway in the Indonesian archipelago. Massacres in various parts of the world now come at a rate of one every three months.

Time is getting short and the old man has gone to greet the sea, but he got into the water like a frightened pet. His childhood beach has become very ugly; they've removed the pile-dwellings and coloured cabins and stolen the sand. They say the wind swept it away but it's not true; it's been used to mix the cement for small blocks of flats on the cheap. Where once there were undulating, lustrous dunes, there's now a yellowish, muddy expanse.

Back from this final trip, he felt the duty to stop off in the city to say hello to friends, and on the street he met the demon who scoffed at him. It wasn't a hallucination but a physical encounter which, naturally, no one believes in. He wasn't a goat and didn't have horns or a tail; he dresses in civilian attire and blends in with the passers-by, even if he wears oversized shoes.

In the country, he generally assumes an animal form—preferably that of a perched bird flapping its wings. But in the city he has human features and the look of a grizzled gentleman who wants to pass unnoticed. For this reason he conceals his cloven hoof in orthopaedic shoes. He doesn't want to scare anyone, only to jeer at those who come within range to stir up trouble and make people harm themselves of their own accord.

He's Mr Hyde as portrayed in a French film, which Giano remembers was well acted by a talented clown. His wickedness consisted in childish faces and tricks, tripping an old man, stealing a blind man's walking stick, snatching a lady's wig or frightening a baby in its cradle with his grimace. With these techniques he provoked dust-ups everywhere, in the city streets and country squares, between domestic walls and in the intimacy of boudoirs.

This is the devil who makes the rounds, in no way similar to the ambiguous harbinger of death in Venice or the sombre mask that commissions the requiem from Amadeus, but equipped with the subtle malice everyone reserves for their next-door neighbours. A malevolence made to measure for the victim and for that reason delectable.

Idiot is a word used to refer to the retarded. But it means 'the innocent'.

October

The old lady with the scythe sometimes swoops unan-
nounced like a bird of prey, and sometimes keeps people
waiting out of coquetry. But now the story is finished, and
who knows why Giano doesn't shorten the time of his own
volition and cut the thread with his own hand.

Out of cowardice, certainly, because he's afraid of the
dark, because he has obligations. But there's also a hidden
reason, which only one person very close to him could
guess. More than anything, attachments matter and resist,
even the lost ones and a single one that remains. You don't
have to be Ecclesiastes to realize that the rest is wind.

Enough words, now let me see some deeds . . .* It's a
famous farewell that, rhetorically, many would like to
make their own but which very few put into practice.
Among those, some have merited admiration, others met
with sympathy, still others suffered condemnation, but no
one has earned respect.

---

* Johann Wolfgang von Goethe, *Faust* I, Prologue (1806).

History can be read as one continuous attempt by human beings to escape their unhappy condition by recourse to all sorts of external and internal remedies. A different social order (revolutions), spiritual elevation or alienation (religions) or technological prostheses which today have the upper hand. But none of these contrivances has achieved its goal, nor can they, because they're but useful or harmful correctives none of which go to the root of the problem.

That's why a final idea is making progress today, which doesn't propose to improve the species but to project it outside itself, raising or burying it in a different dimension, superhuman or subhuman. Where dinosaurs, to avoid extinction, were incapable or too slow to mutate into hippopotami or other creatures, human beings now seek to escape their own skin and nature, transfiguring the fundamentals of the species and its reproduction and the genetic code of the individual.

A biological trip to the moon. They won't make it, just as Baron Münchhausen wasn't able to raise himself off the ground by lifting himself up by his hair (a funny idea). If, on the other hand, they do achieve their aim, it will not be a dignified way for the human race to disappear.

One of the misfortunes of our times is that science is the mistress and art the handmaid. We don't know what Schopenhauer would have thought of sheep cloning but we do know he found the various effects produced in music by major and minor modes (keys) 'magical and astonishing'. Changing a half note, a semitone, the smallest interval, differentiates the minor mode from the major to such an extent that the first conveys anxiety and the second security. It might seem like a Romantic fantasy but it's a message any ear can receive even without knowing where it comes from. Even more curious is that, in their turn, modes in major keys have variable effects, even though they're pythagorically identical. Magical and astonishing like the essential things (the essence of things, that is) which the heart senses and reason mislays.

One says fear of God but not fear of Reason.

It's a cloudy month heralding winter and for that reason dedicated to the dead. The doctor, having rushed to Giano's sickbed, advises him to keep his spirits up without paying any attention to the anniversaries of deaths, three of which fall this month. The doctor doesn't understand that for the elderly the tolling of the bell is a daily occurrence.

Giano knows he's arrived with impunity on the threshold of the year 2000, because he hasn't simply benefited from the dual consciousness everyone is endowed with, but from a multiple consciousness that has favoured his survival beyond good and evil. He has had more than two faces, unlike the homonymous divinity, and his many consciousnesses have alternated with one another like a seesaw.

Now a young immigrant woman informs him that the year with three zeros will witness the end of the world. The young woman is not in any doubt and adds that many people share the same conviction, even if they keep it secret. But she makes a point of clarifying that it will not be a universal judgement since only bad people will die. And she awaits this date with tranquillity because she hasn't done anyone any evil.

Giano doesn't share this certainty, or any others, only a conviction he confides to relatives and friends gathered round the sickbed. He warns them that in no part of the world, and in no corner of creation, do cats with boots exist; and he recommends not believing anyone who claims the contrary.

Before breathing his last, he recites two lines of verse: O fountain mouth, giver, you, mouth, which speaks inexhaustibly of that one, pure thing.* And he leaves written in testament that water is the most beautiful thing in nature—the clear water of springs, the transparent water of streams, the water that fills the amphora and overflows, the water one gathers in the palm of the hand and carries to the lips to quench one's thirst at the close of day.

---

* Rainer Maria Rilke, *Sonnets to Orpheus*, 'XV'.